Elevating
Expectations

Elevating Expectations

Expectations

*A New Take on
Accountability,
Achievement,
and Evaluation*

JoAnn Wong-Kam

Alice K. Kimura

Anna Y. Sumida

Joyce Ahuna-Kaʻaiʻai

Mikilani Hayes Maeshiro

HEINEMANN
Portsmouth, NH

Heinemann
A division of Reed Elsevier Inc.
361 Hanover Street
Portsmouth, NH 03801–3912
www.heinemann.com

Offices and agents throughout the world

The authors and publisher wish to thank those who have generously given permission to reprint borrowed material:

Figure C–6: Adapted from *Multi-Age and More* by Politano and Davies (1994). Used by permission of Peguis Publishers Ltd., Winnipeg, Manitoba, Canada.

Figures 4–1 and C–7, 4–2 and C–8, 4–3 and C–9: Adapted from *Together Is Better* by Davies, Cameron, Politano, and Gregory (1992). Used by permission of Peguis Publishers Ltd., Winnipeg, Manitoba, Canada.

Figures 4–7 and 5–7: Used by permission of the Punahou School, Honolulu, Hawai'i.

Library of Congress Cataloging-in-Publication Data
Elevating expectations : a new take on accountability, achievement, and evaluation /
    JoAnn Wong-Kam . . . [et al.].
        p. cm.
    Includes bibliographical references.
    ISBN 0-325-00390-4 (paper)
    1. Educational evaluation.   2. Education—Standards.   3. Educational accountability.
    I. Wong-Kam, JoAnn.

    LB2822.75 .E43   2001
    379.1'58—dc21   2001026408

Editor: Lois Bridges
Production editor: Lynne Reed
Cover design: Night and Day Design
Manufacturing: Steve Bernier

Printed in the United States of America on acid-free paper
08   07   06   05   04   VP   3   4   5   6

for Kathleen Chang, our friend and inspiration

Contents

Acknowledgments

Hawai'i has a cultural tradition of *'ohana,* or "family," which extends beyond the typical concept of a nuclear family. Like a village, it embraces the concept of community—a group of people who work, share, help, and learn from one another. Most important, the foundations of *'ohana* are built upon caring, supportive, and respectful relationships. With deepest gratitude, we acknowledge our *'ohana,* those who helped to make this book become a reality.

In our search of ways to make assessment meaningful to students and parents, Anne Davies and Colleen Politano were our first guides. They shared their knowledge, helped us see connections, and helped us shape student progress and evaluation into progress folios. Over the years, Anne and Colleen encouraged us to grow, contributed to our work, reviewed our drafts, helped us problem-solve, and, most important, told us it was okay to "adapt, not adopt" their work.

We thank all our students and parents at Kamehameha Elementary School, where our research originated. They were partners in this journey and kept us going with their willingness to risk and learn alongside us. Hundreds of parents gave us written and verbal feedback, through surveys and personal comments, on the process of goalsetting and student-centered assessment.

We especially thank Tammy A'ea's contributions as a parent and colleague. Tammy and her daughter, Kacey, graciously served as a focused case study, allowing us to understand the growth and effects of student goalsetting, self-evaluation, and three-way conferencing longitudinally from kindergarten through sixth grade. Tammy gave us invaluable feedback and a holistic view of how these processes, over time, affect a child's development and responsibility, honor and nurture student potential, make home and school connections meaningful, and deepen and enrich family relationships. Their messages and work samples are woven throughout our book.

We thank fellow teachers Nani Pai and Charlene Christenson, who dared to take the first steps with us. Getting started was a slow and painstaking process, but year after year, as a community of learners, other interested colleagues joined in and experimented, problem-solved in study groups, searched for better ways, shared new ideas, created new formats, and streamlined systems, making this a gradual process of evolution. Our combined efforts remind us of Anne Davies's mantra, "None of us is as smart as all of us!"

Kahele Kukea, principal at Kamehameha Elementary School, made our inquiry possible by allowing us to take risks and break new ground. He trusted us to experiment with authentic assessments, revise report cards, and redesign parent-teacher conferences.

Our research expanded to Punahou School where supervisor Brad Kerwin infused us with energy and a desire to continue developing our ideas. He read early drafts and was a cheerleader for us. We are thankful to the students and parents of Punahou School who continued to make this a successful journey.

We are indebted to the extensive assistance and encouragement of our editor, Lois Bridges, who gently but firmly pointed us in the right direction and guided us to transform our stories so that the true essence about learning and student progress could be shared.

Our friend Regie Routman believed we had a story to share with others and brought our work to Lois. Regie took the time to review our manuscript and offer insightful comments. She continues to give us faith and the will to believe in ourselves as researchers and professionals.

Our mentors, Kathy Au and Jackie Carroll, taught us early in our career what it meant to be teacher researchers. Their early training and collaboration helped us to develop procedures, tasks, and skills for working on this project.

We also thank Diane Stephens and Karen Smith for seeing value and potential in our work. Their early enthusiasm inspired us to move forward to fully develop a manuscript to be published.

Through our journey as teachers and learners, the greatest blessing has been Don Graves, our wise friend, who lit the fire and taught us to connect and learn from the lives and minds of children—the heart of teaching and soul of this book.

Last but not least, we thank our husbands and families who patiently gave us the time to devote long hours to this project.

'Ike aku, 'ike mai, kōkua aku kōkua mai;
pela iho la ka nohona 'ohana.

Recognize and be recognized, help and be helped,
such is family life.

—Pukui 1983, 130

Introduction

JoAnn Wong-Kam

It's nine o'clock on a Saturday morning. At a time when most people are relaxing at home or out enjoying the weekend, twenty-one elementary teachers from various public and private schools on Oahu are gathered in a first-grade classroom to learn. They started meeting a year ago to support each other in improving classroom assessment and evaluation practices. Alice Kimura facilitates this group of teachers learning from other teachers. She listens to their questions, plans agendas, searches out resources, and shares her own experiences.

Over sushi, pastries, and juice, the teachers share their struggles.

"How do I get started? No one at my school is doing anything like this. I don't know what to do."

"I've tried some things but don't know what to do next."

"I've collected all kinds of student work. What do I do with all this stuff?"

"My students can't self-evaluate. They don't understand what to do when I say 'tell me how you are doing.' How do we get kids to be reflective?"

The colleagues also share their successes. Forms are exchanged, student samples are reviewed, progress folios are displayed, and teachers tell their stories. It will take time, but these teachers are involved in something that can change the way they teach and look at children.

This book is the result of our work with children, and the changes it has meant for us as teachers. We see children as independent learners with ideas and goals of their own. We talk with children and parents as partners in learning. We assess and evaluate student progress with their ideas and perspectives—as well as their parents'—alongside our own.

It would have been overwhelming for me to try and formulate a student-centered assessment and evaluation process on my own. I was fortunate to work with colleagues who had the same commitment to giving students ownership of their learning. The process we share in this book came from experiences in our classrooms and with our students and their parents, and from many hours of talk. We were all teachers at an elementary school in Honolulu, Hawai'i. Anna Sumida, then a kindergarten teacher, taught five-year-olds about goals and used teacher-student interviews as beginning steps in self-assessment. Joyce Ahuna-Ka'ai'ai, introduced the voices of her second graders into conversations as she brought students and parents together for goalsetting and celebrations of learning. Alice Kimura, an experienced third-grade teacher, mapped out for us a step-by-step process for getting young children through the arduous task of evidence selection, self-reflection, and conference preparation. Miki Maeshiro, a sixth-grade teacher, opened our eyes to see how upper-elementary students actively took control of their learning and evaluation and played it against their growing understanding of who they were and who they wanted to be.

I, JoAnn Wong-Kam, was a participant, observer, facilitator, and the recorder for this project, which began during the 1994–1995 school year and continues today as we gain new insights from our students. We often share our work-in-progress with other educators who are searching for a "better way" to teach children. Their questions give us a new lens for looking at our process and revising it. The adaptations they make to our model improve our ability to gather information and meet the needs of students.

This book shares the processes and procedures that, through trial and error, brings kindergarteners through sixth graders full circle, from setting goals and plans of action to reflecting on progress made and setting new goals. We describe what has worked in our student-centered classrooms, where "we respond to what the child is trying to do" (Smith 1984, 24) with our teaching, assessment, and evaluation. Student-led conferences and the progress folio process helped students and families plan and direct a course of personal development, elevating expectations for everyone. This book is written with the hope that it will give you a new take on accountability, achievement, and evaluation. By bringing together students, parents, and teachers, we make learning an exciting and successful experience for all of us.

1

Children First

- How Children Learn
- Making the Change
- Children Take Ownership

How Children Learn

It was the day before Halloween, and the students had brought in pumpkins for carving jack-o'-lanterns. Before carving, we estimated the pumpkins' weight and circumference: "How big around?" Then we chose one of their pumpkins and gathered the twenty-four eager first graders around a large tub of water, and posed a question: "What will happen if we put the pumpkin in the tub of water?"

Danny's hand shot up. "It will sink, it will sink!"

Mary explained. "It's heavy so it will sink in the water."

"Okay, let's find out." I handed Mary the pumpkin, and while her classmates squirmed with excitement, she lowered the pumpkin into the tub. Lo and behold, the pumpkin floated! What happened?

Jimmy, recalling his experiences with jack-o'-lanterns, figured it out. "The pumpkin is hollow inside!"

"Yes, yes!" agreed Victor, "It has air inside! That's why it floated."

Let's step back for a moment and consider what happened here. As students took in new information—that a heavy but hollow object will float—they had to modify their previous understanding—that heavy things sink—with their new experience. In other words, new learning occurred. We cannot begin our conversation about a student-teacher-parent collaborative approach to evaluation without first

1

discussing how children learn. Once we understand the learning process, we can align ourselves with a method of assessment and evaluation that supports and nurtures learning. For this discussion, we will consider two basic models of learning and teaching.

One model of learning is the *empty vessel* analogy. Children are viewed as passive learners who come to school as empty vessels, which we then proceed to fill each year with important facts. Children progress up the academic ladder, accumulating more and more facts. In this traditional framework, schooling amounts to the transmission of a body of knowledge from the teacher or text to the learner (Strickland and Strickland 2000). If this is our view of the learning and teaching process, then the evaluation system we adopt will be equally simple: We determine how many facts our students have collected and memorized. Standardized tests, which evaluate learning as the accumulation of facts, provide a measure of teaching-learning success.

The second model reflects a constructivist educators' point of view, most widely represented by John Dewey (1938, 1963), Jean Piaget (1954), and Lev Vygotsky (1978). In this model, learners are actively engaged in learning, constructing, and creating their own understandings of the world. As active learners, they evaluate new or unfamiliar experiences by comparing them with previous learning encounters. As they discover similarities and differences, students revise, refine, and extend their understanding. They are continually constructing their own unique view of the world based on a wide range of incoming learning data from seemingly infinite sources. What's more, learning is highly influenced by the learner's relationships with other learners. The feedback they receive from others regarding their ideas and behaviors either reinforces their understandings or causes them to question and alter their beliefs. Learning is highly social, influenced and shaped through interactions with others, particularly the child's family.

This view of learning expects students to do more than just memorize facts. Constructivists want "students to take responsibility for their own learning, to be autonomous thinkers, to develop integrated understandings of concepts, and to pose—and seek to answer—important questions" (Brooks and Brooks 1993, 1999). In other words, students are not simply "empty vessels to be filled" but engaged learners driven to learn to satisfy their own compelling curiosity about the world around them. Learning begins with questions that the children themselves are inspired to answer.

Constructivists also tend to believe that learning develops in multiple ways and may manifest itself through multiple modalities. Howard Gardner's theory of multiple intelligences (1983) challenges us to look at our potential for knowing beyond our capacity for language (verbal/linguistic intelligence) or deductive/inductive reasoning, numbers, and patterns (mathematical/logical intelligence).

Gardner maintains that we would do well to consider a range of intelligences:

- *intrapersonal intelligence*: related to knowing oneself, one's emotions and thinking processes, awareness of spiritual realities
- *interpersonal intelligence*: related to working cooperatively and communicating with others
- *visual/spatial intelligence*: related to the visualization of objects and the creation of internal mental images
- *body/kinesthetic intelligence*: related to physical movement
- *musical/rhythmic intelligence*: related to tones, rhythms, and beats.

Jason, a sixth grader in remedial reading, stands before his classmates to present his project on surfing. An expert on the subject, he explains clearly how he prepares his board with wax before going out into the waves. Later, Kalei brings out her hula implements as she describes how dancers use each one. She closes her presentation with a dance using the *'uli'uli*, "feather gourd rattle."

Although these two students were struggling readers, when given the opportunity to *show* what they did know and to *highlight* their strengths, we could recognize and appreciate Jason's body/kinesthetic intelligence and Kalei's musical/rhythmic skills.

Once we accept that intelligence is not a singular entity, we can recognize the many potentials that exist in all learners and provide opportunities for learning and expressing understanding in new ways. What's more, we can offer numerous ways in which our students can express their new learning and understanding, including dance, drama, and creative movement. These art, music, and visualization activities are important because they bring students' understandings to deeper levels. Students are able to see and represent their ideas in more than one way.

In order to link our understanding of effective teaching and learning with assessment and evaluation, we want to select methods of assessment that recognize the multiple dimensions of knowing that students can exhibit. Therefore, we want to select and evaluate a rich and complex range of the *artifacts* of our students' learning: writing samples, artwork, photographs, research projects, and other examples of actual performance and achievement. These artifacts, our students' *proof of learning*, far transcend simple numerical test scores or letter grades. Our ultimate goal as evaluators is always to improve student learning. Evaluation should help us help our students learn more.

Making the Change

Making the change from traditional models of assessment and evaluation to a student-centered approach takes time, patience, support, and hard work. For teachers, it means:

- Know what's important in teaching and learning.
- Find out what children know and can do.
- Trust children and give them time to learn.
- Take time to learn, reflect, and refine teaching practices.

Know What's Important in Teaching and Learning

It is easy to get confused and distracted in our teaching. We look at the number of objectives on scope-and-sequence charts in curriculum manuals, then add to that the standards and other school mandates that we are asked to comply with, and we feel overwhelmed. We must remember that we are educators, and the word *educate* comes from the Greek word *edos,* which means "educe" or "draw out." We need to draw or bring out the potential in our children rather than fill them with meaningless facts and drill them with countless worksheets. We need to refocus ourselves on what really matters in our classrooms.

Take time to think about what our children need to become independent, lifelong learners, who are confident and caring members of a community. List all the ideas you can think of, then review them to look for connections. Categorize similar thoughts by grouping them together and labeling them. What big ideas emerge? Do you begin to see your goals more clearly?

With colleagues, we discussed our literacy goals for our students. When they leave our classes, we want our students to:

- Enjoy reading and know something about literature and authors so they can choose their own books to read. Unfortunately, we know too many children who will read only when assigned to. Then, when given the freedom to select their own books, they are not able to make their own choice.
- Connect their reading to their lives and experiences and reach a deeper understanding of the world around them. Our study of Louise Rosenblatt's reader response theory showed us that text does not carry meaning in itself— meaning is constructed between literature and the reader. "Reading is a transaction, a two-way process, involving a reader and a text" (Rosenblatt 1993). Too often in our past teaching experiences we treated books as if there were one message, lesson, or theme that students were expected to identify. The search for the *right answer* cut short any possibilities of students finding their own meaning. They read to meet the teacher's purpose.
- Feel confident about their writing. We have done much work with process writing (Graves 1983, 1994) and believe it's best to begin with writing topics that our students find significant—to explore topics that interest

4

them or that they already know a lot about. In this way, students find their "voices." Our writing workshops create opportunities for the meaningful teaching of skills and conventions. They also create an enjoyment and enthusiasm for writing that story starters and assigned topics had previously diminished.

- Use reading and writing to pursue their own interests. Using the power of inquiry, not only do our students learn to be problem *solvers*, investigating questions we pose for them, but also to be problem *posers*, searching for ideas to answer their own wonderings (Short, Harste, and Burke 1996). We believe students should be able to follow the learning path of their own curiosity; accordingly, we realize that we need to help them develop the skills and knowledge to do this successfully.

By focusing on what we feel is important for our children to learn and achieve, we set the stage for changes in other aspects of our classrooms.

Find Out What Children Know and Can Do

It is easy to blame children for poor performance in our schools. To take the focus off the teaching and point fingers at students, we often hear comments such as "they don't try hard enough," "they can't remember anything I tell them," or "they don't want to learn." We label children too quickly as *attention deficit, learning disabled,* or *dyslexic,* so we can explain away their failure. If we truly believe that every child can learn, then we must look deeply at our children and listen hard to them, focusing on and celebrating their strengths before addressing their weaknesses.

Take time to observe children, to become *kidwatchers,* as Yetta Goodman would say. A kidwatcher is a teacher who knows how to carefully observe her students while they are engaged in learning and then determine what they know and what they still need to know so she can provide the sensitive, thoughtful instruction that gently nudges them forward on their developmental learning path. Kidwatching is an invaluable assessment skill, but it takes time to learn; as Regie Routman (1991, 1994) reminds us:

> Before we can become expert observers, we have to be expert learners. We have to be able to observe [our students] and value [their] strengths more than deficits. We have to know what to look for: what are the developmental markers we are seeing or not seeing? We have to be expert listeners: what does the student really mean? We have to be able to recognize an individual student's learning patterns and use them to take the child further. (30)

We want children to be able to show us what they know and what they can do, so we need to gather assessment data and concretely document our students' learning in a variety of ways. Anne Davies (2000) and Lois Bridges (1995) identify three things, discussed below, that we can do to document learning.

Watch Children in Action (Observation of Process) As students acquire and process new information, we observe how they use their prior knowledge to make sense of new experiences. We look for the skills and strategies they use in working out problems and answering questions. Bridges (1995, 29) suggests that we take note of their

engagement

- pleasure: confidence and involvement in the learning event
- perseverance: working for extended periods of time
- risk-taking: curiosity and inventiveness
- responsibility: effective use of time; completing projects in a timely way

collaboration

- ability to share ideas and opinions with peers, teachers, and other adults
- willingness to seek and respond to feedback from peers, teachers, and other adults
- willingness to use input from peers or teachers
- ability to undertake a task for and with a group

flexibility

- ability to explore and use multiple learning modalities
- exercising options: moving from one modality to another
- problem solving: using many resources in search for answers to questions
- willingness to revise: deciding how, when, and why changes be made.

Look at Collections of Children's Work (Observation of Product) Students can take responsibility for brainstorming and collecting the evidence that shows their progress toward learning goals. When children show what they know through products or presentations, we get a good picture of what they have learned. We can look for

- understanding of content
- conventions and forms
- presentation: clarity, focus, voice
- detail
- purpose (Bridges 1995, 29–30)

Talk with and Listen to Children (Conversations, Conferences, and Reflections) Sometimes we need to talk with our students to truly understand the reasons for the choices they make and what they think about various learning experiences. While writing self-reflections is valuable, younger children may not be able to reveal all their thoughts in writing, but would be happy to tell you about them. Whether we conference with students or have them write down their reflections, here are questions to consider for students and teachers:

Questions for the student

- What can I do? What do I want to do?
- What do I know? What do I want to know?
- What will I do next?

Questions for the teacher

- What strengths does the learner have?
- What needs does the learner have?
- How can I help? (Bridges 1995, 30)

Trust Children and Give Them Time to Learn

We often feel pressured to put curriculum objectives ahead of student needs. We don't have time for children to discover the connections or assimilate the facts, so we tell them what they need to know. We lecture and then test them on the required information. However, this runs counter to our beliefs about student-centered learning. Students need time

> to make connections within their own thoughts; time to actively discover relatedness among events; time for expressing, questioning, likening, remembering, appreciating, enjoying, discerning, and imagining that leads to the development of deep understanding." (Falk 2000, 158)

We need to give them the time.

Often when we share the idea of students participating in assessment and evaluation, skeptics question whether students really have the ability to be honest evaluators of their own work. When we show them the progress folios and read the students' own words about their goals and progress, they are eager to try it with their class. But to participate successfully in assessment and evaluation, children need time to learn the process with the teacher's careful guidance. The amount of help the teacher provides changes to match the needs of the learner, something Vygotsky calls *scaffolding*. More help is provided when a child first approaches a new learning task, and less help is needed later when the child has had the time to experiment, explore, and practice and become more proficient (Au, Carroll, and Scheu 1997, 15).

At the beginning of the year, we use prompts and many examples to help students understand goals. Chapter 2 describes the different ways we have introduced goalsetting with our elementary students.

We use *think alouds* to demonstrate how we evaluate what we do well—our strengths—compared to what we need help with—our challenges. We gather the students around us at the end of a work period, and ask,

> What went well today?
> What do we need to work on more?
> What do we need to do make things better?

For example, if this discussion were held after a third-grade writing workshop, students might share how they enjoyed writing their stories, but felt the time was too short. So, the decision could be made to extend the writing workshop period by at least fifteen minutes. These discussions allow the teacher to get feedback from students, and it also helps the students to see how reflecting on their work can lead to changes and improvements.

Teachers can also spend time conferencing with students as needed to provide feedback on progress toward goals. In a fifth-grade reading conference, for example, a teacher and student review the student's reading log, a list of books selected by students for recreational reading.

> TEACHER: What was your goal for this term?
> STUDENT: To find new books to read, because I usually only choose nonfiction books.
> TEACHER: On your reading log, I see you are reading *Shiloh*. What do you think of that book?
> STUDENT: I really like it because I like dogs. I'd like to find more stories about dogs after this.
> TEACHER: You are working on your goals and are reading some good chapter books now.

Gradually, with feedback from the teacher and additional experiences evaluating their own work against rubrics (see Chapter 5), students learn to take ownership of their learning.

Take Time to Learn, Reflect, and Refine Teaching Practices

Adapt, not adopt. Anne Davies shared this wise advice with us. There are so many ideas to choose from, and we can wear ourselves out trying to implement changes in our teaching too fast. We need to look at what is available and makes sense to us, then try one thing at a time. We will often feel frustrated when things do not go smoothly—we are putting ourselves at risk and it makes us uncomfortable. So we reflect on what we have tried, make changes, and try again. Experimenting to find the best strategies for use with our students takes time and can't be rushed. However, it can be made easier by finding colleagues to work with and reading professional literature to expand our knowledge base, not just in assessment but also in language arts and the content areas. Effective teaching evolves through continuous reflection, revision, and self-evaluation.

Children Take Ownership

It's the end of the school year and the children prepare to take home their progress folios. Each progress folio's pages are filled with evidence of growth—reading logs, literature responses, mathematics problems, poetry, research reports. The students gather in small groups around the classroom to share their folios, often smiling and laughing at their early samples.

"Did I really write like that?"

"Look at all the mistakes I made. I didn't know my math facts then."

"Wow, I really read a lot of books!"

"I really worked hard this year."

They have come a long way since September. We know it, but more important, they know it, and have proof to show of their hard work. Below are comments written by students at the end of second grade.

Beth

As a learner, I read with expression. When I read I make life connections between the book I am reading and myself. As a writer, I am proud because I put quality ideas into my writing. I think my writing is wonderful because I can do so many different kinds of writing.

Kathy

The most important thing I am trying to do well is my writing. This is important to me because I need to put more detail and feeling into my work.

Conroy

I have been reading more chapter books now. I enjoy reading. If my mother said to read for thirty minutes, I can do it. As a writer, I can put my ideas down. I can write almost anything.

Julie

As a reader, I have become much better and can read chapter books now! I think I've become much better because I've learned to choose better authors and books. I know I've come a long way in reading!

When students write evaluations about themselves with such details and feelings, we sense the ownership they have over their learning. They acknowledge their strengths while also identifying things that challenge them. From their self-evaluations, students set goals, make action plans, and look over their work for signs of progress. This all occurs within classrooms where they receive encouragement from their teachers and classmates. These students are able to bring their successes and struggles before their parents, and enlist their support. Schooling is now a collaborative venture among parents, teachers, and students. Children have added their voice to the conversation.

Assessment is meaningful when it reflects the learning going on and informs both the student and the teacher so that each can refine and extend learning. Let's take a closer look at the process that enables us to become learning partners with our students. Chapter 2 investigates how effective assessment and evaluation begins with specific, instruction-oriented goals and action plans.

2

Bridging Learning Goals and Instruction

Assessment and Evaluation in the Classroom

- What Matters in Literacy Teaching and Learning?
- How Do We Set Meaningful Goals with Children?
- How Do We Use Action Plans to Meet Goals?
- How Do We Connect Instruction to Goals?

It's September, and parents are at school for open house. In Joyce Ahuna-Kaʻaiʻaiʻs second-grade classroom there is a *Me museum*, where each student has set up a display of three or four items telling something about him or her. Soccer awards, family photos, artwork, pictures of pets, and favorite books are some of the things the students have carefully chosen to represent themselves. Prior to setting up the display, each child shared their treasures with their classmates so they could get to know one another. For the open house display, the students wrote descriptions of themselves and the items for the visiting parents.

There is much conversation as the visitors walk around looking at each display. Joyce moves among them, introducing herself. She approaches Kyle's parents, standing at his display, when Kyle's mother comments, "Look at how neat the other children's handwriting is. Kyle's writing is so messy. Linda's display is so neat and she writes so much. Kyle hardly wrote anything."

Joyce realizes that she needs to help Kyle's parents see he brings other strengths to school—ones that cannot be judged from just one piece of writing.

"Kyle knows so much about books," she says. "He talks about the stories you read together at home. He is such an enthusiastic learner, and is trying hard to get his ideas down in writing. He has a great attitude."

Joyce knows that helping parents see what their child can do is one of the first steps in building her partnership with parents and their children.

What Matters in Literacy Teaching and Learning?

Comments from parents reveal a lot about what they understand and value in their child's education. Comparisons to other students are often made based on neatness, spelling, and quantity of work completed. Students are influenced by their parents' perceptions, and label themselves as *good students*, *poor students*, or *just plain lazy*. So it is important that we, as teachers, clearly communicate our beliefs and goals, so both students and parents know what we striving for, and how they can then strive to meet those expectations. We want to move beyond just the *outward appearance* of learning and develop parents' and students' understanding of what matters in our literacy teaching and learning.

Helping students become confident learners means that we must identify the behaviors, attitudes, skills, strategies, and knowledge that our students need to be successful. We need goals for teaching and learning that go beyond scope-and-sequence charts. Furthermore, we need to share this information with parents so they can understand the role they play in supporting their children's growth.

What should our students know and be able to do as effective readers and writers? What is important for us to emphasize in literacy teaching and learning? Too often we focus on the activities, the topics, or the skills without a true understanding of what these mean for the students. In the short time we have with our class, are we trying to cover a curriculum that is a mile wide and an inch deep? Teachers must take the responsibility for choosing what to teach, how to teach it, and for explaining why it is important for the students to learn it. Reflecting and identifying our goals and beliefs allow us to wisely choose the curriculum and strategies that meet the needs of our students.

In our teacher group, we shared our beliefs and goals for reading and writing with each other, ideas based on our experiences with children and our knowledge of reading and writing. Taking the time to talk about our ideas and listen to one another generated questions such as "Was that idea only important for upper elementary students?" "What ideas matter across the grades?" "How does that look with first graders compared to sixth graders?" We then selected a few broad belief and goal statements for reading and writing that we could all focus on, listed below.

Reading Goals

- Students should be able to read, comprehend, and respond critically to what they read.
- Students should have choices in what they read.
- Students should be able to read for sustained periods of time.
- Students should read a variety of literature.

- Students should have strategies for figuring out unfamiliar words.
- Students should enjoy reading.

Writing Goals

- Students should be able to communicate thoughts, ideas, and feelings effectively when they write.
- Students should have choices when they write.
- Students should be able to write for sustained periods of time.
- Students should be able to write for a variety of purposes and audiences.
- Students should have the skills to write well.
- Students should enjoy writing.

What did these goals look like in our classrooms? From kindergarten to sixth grade, good readers talk about books with excitement, sharing titles and sometimes exchanging books with others. They read all kinds of literature, including sports stories, mysteries, and informational texts, as well as newspapers. They make regular visits to the library, where avid readers often ask for recommendations from the librarians. Good readers have an appetite for reading and can be found with a book whenever they have a free moment. Children in kindergarten know the work of Eric Carle and Leo Lionni. Second and third graders can identify Cynthia Rylant and Dick King-Smith as two of their favorite authors. In the upper elementary classrooms, Katherine Patterson, Jack Gantos, and J. K. Rowling are popular.

In our literature discussions the good readers go beyond the plot lines and share the ideas they get from the author's work. They bring their personal experiences to their reading. For these students, reading is a "transaction" (Rosenblatt 1993) or two-way process between them and the story. They create unique interpretations as the experiences of the characters come together with their own personal stories. Teachers nurture these connections in literature discussions so that students can "live inside the world of story in ways that transform their thinking about their lives and the world" (Short 1997, 25).

Writing often does not generate the same enthusiasm as reading. In fact, many students are frustrated writers—they don't know what to write about, how to express their ideas, or even want to write. When this happens, we share stories of our lives by bringing in objects that hold some meaning for us. One teacher brought in some turquoise and sterling silver earrings that she received as a gift from a Navajo tribe she had visited in New Mexico. She explained to her students how each time she looked at the earrings she could feel the warm, dry air, and hear the beating of drums and the slow rhythmic chanting of the Navajo singers. Other teachers read stories about families and pets, and make links to their lives with stories that begin, "I had a dog once that was like that," or "My grandma is just like the one in the story because once she . . . ." We find the stories in our own lives, then write them down so they won't be forgotten. This is how we help our students find meaning and pleasure in writing.

We want our students to become good writers, so we write with them almost every day, trying to make our ideas clear, learning writing techniques that make our words come to life. We work on the process of writing as well as the craft of writing (Fletcher 1993), developing our description, dialogue, action, and characters. Writing is hard work and needs a lot of support. We share ideas together as a class, conference in small groups, and encourage each other. We find good examples of writing in the literature we read and emulate our favorite authors. At the end of the year, we have grown as writers because we have worked and lived like writers.

In our minds we can see connections between our goals and our instruction, but do our students see these same qualities for achieving success as readers and writers? Figure 2–1 illustrates ideas shared by a second-grade class of what they know about good readers.

In JoAnn's fifth-grade class, students identified similar characteristics. It was interesting to see how they were able to group the ideas around key points when asked if they could notice any relationships among the different ideas:

TIM: Yeah, *take notes* and *show thinking* kind of go together.

JoANN: Can anyone say why would you put them together?

KAREN: I think Tim put them together because you have to understand what you are reading before you can take notes or show thinking.

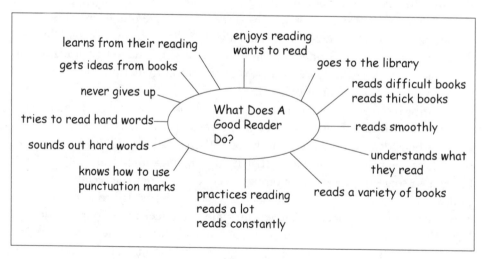

Figure 2–1. Good Reader Chart for Grade 2.

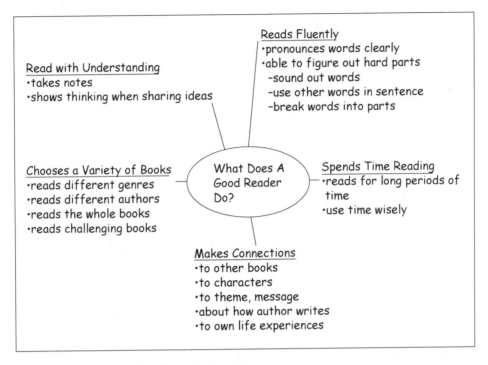

Figure 2–2. Good Reader Chart for Grade 5.

JoAnn: Let's put them together and call it 'read with understanding' for now. Anyone notice anything else that seems to be similar?

The discussion continued with other students sharing their insights and reasons. Figure 2–2 shows what the final class chart looked like.

Similar charts were created from class discussions around the question "What do good writers do?" The students' ideas were webbed randomly on chart paper, then reorganized by the children so similar ideas were grouped together. Figure 2–3 shows a chart from a second-grade class.

These charts should remain in clear view on the classroom wall for the year to remind us, and our students, what matters as readers.

Often, there are students who are not sure what makes someone a good reader—in their view, either you are a good reader or you aren't. These students could offer some broad statements such as "Good readers like to read" or "Good readers read a lot of books." Neither the specific skills and behaviors nor the opportunity to become better readers were part of their literacy experiences.

In order to help them understand, we start with whatever ideas the students give us, and then throughout the day we highlight the good things they do as readers.

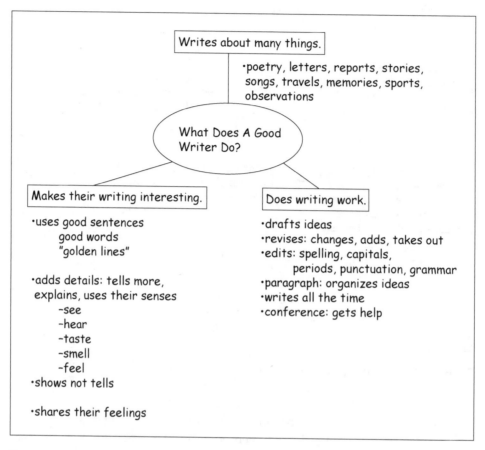

Figure 2–3. Good Writer Chart for Grade 2.

After Sustained Silent Reading period, for example, we praise the students: "The room was so silent today, you must have found some great books to read. That's something that good readers do—enjoy reading." After Read Aloud when children share their questions or comments about the day's story, we remember to point out, "Those are all wonderful ideas. It shows that you were really thinking about the story. That's what good readers do." When students bring books to share in our Sharing Circle, we let them know that "Good readers read often and even share what they read with others." As students recognize that these behaviors and skills help them improve as readers, we add them to a Good Readers chart—a cumulative record of what we notice in reading.

In writing workshop, we take advantage of sharing times to point out when students use interesting words or add details to help us picture their stories in our minds. "These are things that good writers do," we say to them. If a child has a hard time finding a topic to write about, we brainstorm ideas together or review previously written ideas in their notebooks to find something they can work on. "All writers get stuck and need help thinking of what to write," we say. "That is a goal for many of us as writers."

By providing opportunities for students to recognize the many things they do throughout the day, we help them articulate what good readers and writers do. We continue to build this knowledge throughout the year and add ideas to our classroom charts. These charts help all of us to identify and set learning goals. Through this process, students take a more active part in assessment and take responsibility for their learning.

How Do We Set Meaningful Goals with Children?

When introducing the word *goal* to our students, it helps to use a recognizable connection such as sports. The children might say:

> "When I play soccer, we have to kick the ball into the goal and it's the goalie's job to protect the goal."

> "In football the players have to get the football over the goal line."

Alice Kimura's third graders would share their fitness goals for PE class, and how a goal was something they wanted to get better at by practicing: "I want to be able to climb higher on the pegboard, but I have a lot of practicing to do before I can reach that goal."

With the younger children in her kindergarten class, Anna Sumida found that a demonstration was helpful in explaining goal setting. She set up three plastic bowling pins on the carpet, and explained that her *goal* was to knock down all three pins with the plastic ball she held in her hands. Postures straightened, eyes widened, and grinning faces anxiously awaited her attempt to roll. She asked, "Who thinks I will reach my goal?" Unanimously, all the children raised their hands and began cheering for her.

Standing seven feet away from the pins, Anna threw the ball. It curved to the left and missed all three pins. Everyone squirmed and giggled, and some begged to do it for her. She quickly asked, "Did I reach my goal?"

"Noooo!"

After two more attempts, she finally toppled the three pins.

"Now you reached your goal," congratulated Wilson.

This example led to further discussion of goals and how to determine if they were met. By the end of the talk, each child had set a goal he or she wanted to achieve by the end of the day, including "Eat everything on my plate at lunch today," "Jump rope ten times without stopping," and "Try not to get caught when we play chase master at recess."

During lunch, many of the children showed Anna their clean plates. Others verified jump rope goals for one another. By the end of the day, most of the kindergartners had reached their goals. Making short-term goals and evaluating if they had been met went on for several weeks before setting long-term goals for reading and writing.

Anna did a great deal in setting up her classroom to support reading and writing development. Her students were immersed in wonderful reading experiences through read alouds, literature discussions, and shared reading experiences, as well as daily reading and writing projects. She modeled what readers and writers did, thinking aloud through the steps they would need to take.

Her students then began to articulate what "good readers do." They were developing an understanding of appropriate early reading behaviors.

What Good Readers Do

- Look at the pictures so you know what the book will be about.
- Don't make up a word—think of what would make sense.
- Sound out words.
- Read books to friends.
- Practice reading at home.
- Read books you like.
- Read when you have free time.
- Point to words as you read.
- Correct words if you read them wrong.

In their second- and third-grade classrooms, Joyce and Alice found it helpful to have students plan weekly goals and then evaluate to see if they had met their goals at the end of the week. Each day, students would copy the schedule of that day's activities on their Weekly Progress sheet (see Chapter 3 and Appendix C). On Monday, students would set the goal they would work on for that week. One third grader's goal was to complete his work on time. Another student knew she needed to pay attention to the teacher when she talks, so that became her goal. At the end of each day, students took a few minutes to reflect on how their day went and wrote a comment on their assignment sheet. Then at the end of the week they would summarize how they felt about their efforts toward achieving their goal.

After introducing the concept of goals to our students, we want them to focus on specific goals related to their literacy development. We might ask, "What would you like to learn to do in order to become better readers? What would you like to learn to do in order to become better writers?" Helping young students to answer these questions takes patience and practice. Here is what Joyce learned about goalsetting with her second graders:

> I remember we would discuss what made excellent readers and writers. We would identify those characteristics and write them on charts. From there the children would pick what they thought would help them become better readers and writers. Sometimes they would choose very broad, perhaps unattainable goals. My dilemma was, should I guide them to something more appropriate, or do I let them go through their own discovery? There was Constance, who wanted to write a chapter book in four weeks. Her own discovery of choosing an unattainable goal was more powerful than if I had suggested a goal for her. The next time she chose a goal, she had a better idea of what she could achieve.

Older students, like the sixth graders in Miki Maeshiro's class, have an easier time setting specific reading and writing goals for themselves. They understand that goals take time to achieve and require commitment and hard work. For example, Blake wants to read regularly for an hour a day; Nadine wants to use her five senses more in her writing, and increase her vocabulary; Ken wants to use *touching* words to get the reader's attention. Miki's careful articulation about what makes good readers and writers in sixth grade are reflected in her students' goals.

When we show our students what matters in learning, and allow them to choose what they want to work on, we give them a voice in their learning. Students see that they matter in our classrooms. Next, we help them work toward their goals by identifying the steps they can take to get there. These steps, or *action plans*, make goals less abstract and more attainable.

How Do We Use Action Plans to Meet Goals?

Jane Hansen, and her work with the Manchester Project (1998), taught us that it is important to ask, "What would you like to learn to do to become a better reader?" and then "How do you intend to do that?" This second question guides students toward understanding that they have a better chance of achieving goals if they identify the steps needed to get there.

Asking students what they will do to achieve goals is often a difficult question for students to answer without some prompting from the teacher, such as:

- What can you do to work toward your goal?
- What actions can you take?
- What can the teacher do to help you?
- What can your parents do to help you?
- What can we do as a class to help you?

19

Name: Kealii	Date: 9/28

Goal:
   To write a better reading
   response.
	Goal:
	   Write in my notebook more
	   often.

Plan:
  1. Write a better summary.
  2. Make more corrections.
	Plan:
	  1. Take my notebook home.
	  2. Write more memories.

Figure 2–4. Goal and Action Plan for First-Grade Student.

If a student's goal is to read harder books, a plan of action might include going to the library more often and asking the librarian for help selecting books. If the goal is to spend more time reading, a student could set a schedule with his or her parents for more time to read at home.

Students from grade 2 through grade 6 write down their goals and plans on a goal sheet, which is taped to their desks as a reminder of what they are working on. (An example of a first grader's goal and action plan is shown in Figure 2–4.) Teachers refer to the goal sheets as needed, but they also keep a separate class list of goals and action plans.

Kendall, a fifth grader, was an average student who did well in mathematics but found reading anything above a third-grade level difficult. On a self-evaluation sheet filled out at the end of the second quarter, he wrote, "I still need to improve on my reading. Sometimes I don't understand what I read." His new goals were to read more books and to understand what he read. When Kendall met with his teacher in conference to review his goals, she asked how he planned to work toward his goal. Kendall answered that he would set a regular time to read each night, and that keeping a reading log would help him keep track of his progress. (As part of their regular routine, Kendall's teacher had the students keep a reading log, recording title, author, date, and number of pages read.) To help support his goal of understanding what he read, Kendall's teacher offered to have regular reading conferences to talk about what he was reading. Kendall agreed that these conferences would help him.

When it came to areas of great difficulty, which reading was for Kendall, his teacher found that she needed to take more responsibility for setting up and supporting his action plan. Kendall followed through by spending time in daily individual reading conferences. When these goals were shared with Kendall's parents, they were eager to help.

Once the goals and plans are set up, we help students be mindful of them by posting lists on their desks, keeping a class list at our desks, and giving them copies to post on the refrigerator at home. Teachers can also support students by commenting when they notice them following their action plan:

"I see more books on your reading log. You are remembering your goal of reading more."

"You really asked some good questions in literature circle today. I can see you understand what you read. You must be following your action plan."

Without these subtle reminders, students often forget their goals and don't follow through on their plans. To successfully meet the goals, we need parents, teachers, and at times other students to provide encouragement and assistance with action plans. As teachers, we have another responsibility to ensure success for our students: to connect our instruction with their goals.

How Do We Connect Instruction to Goals?

Finding a way to support goals for twenty-five or more students may seem an almost impossible task. However, as is the case with many of our students, the process is manageable because they focus on three or four main reading or writing goals. For example, in one third-grade classroom, the students' reading goals centered on the following three areas:

- making good reading choices
- improving word reading skills
- developing better reading habits

For writing, the students showed an interest in working on these three goals:

- writing longer stories
- making stories more interesting with details and descriptions
- improving spelling

Although the students choose to work on these goals, we emphasize a balance of good reading and writing behaviors, highlighting the areas selected by students when appropriate. In this way, we continue to improve students' skills and strategies in both strong and weak areas.

One third-grade teacher set up her language arts period so that her students had opportunities to work on their goals (see Figure 2–5). She began the period with writing workshop, where the children had time for writing or sharing their pieces.

21

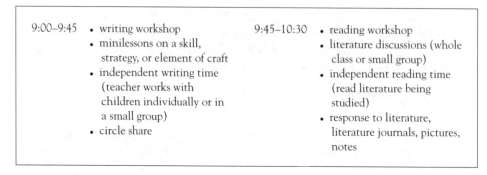

| 9:00–9:45 | • writing workshop
• minilessons on a skill, strategy, or element of craft
• independent writing time (teacher works with children individually or in a small group)
• circle share | 9:45–10:30 | • reading workshop
• literature discussions (whole class or small group)
• independent reading time (read literature being studied)
• response to literature, literature journals, pictures, notes |

Figure 2–5. Language Arts Period.

Sometimes, the workshop began with short focused lessons on a particular skill or element of craft. These minilessons included sharing strategies for brainstorming ideas, adding details, description, dialogue, or action, writing good leads or endings, and choosing a good title. Many students asked for help with spelling, so she spent a few minutes teaching a word family pattern, demonstrating prefixes and root words, or reinforcing other spelling strategies. As students practiced these skills, the teacher pointed out how they were working toward their goal of becoming better spellers.

The teacher circulated around the classroom, going over problems, praising good work, or nudging children to take next steps with their writing by trying to find stronger words or adding description which could help the reader picture the scene better. Having the children's goals listed on a clipboard for easy review helped her link the work students were doing with goals they had set.

Following writing workshop, the students moved into reading workshop, which centered around various literature study activities such as reading, small group discussions with the teacher, or writing or drawing reading responses. This particular third-grade teacher divided her class into three literature groups, with whom she met daily for a literature discussion. Her role in these discussions was to help students talk about characters, events, and themes, as well as to help them make connections to other literature or their own personal experiences. (With older students, the teacher is often a participant, letting students direct the literature conversations.)

During discussions, the teacher might suggest meaningful connections to the literature, while also allowing her students to explore issues and ideas of interest to them. This links her instruction to her students' goals, one of which was to improve understanding of what they read. Other activities related to this goal include written responses, creating webs of important ideas, drawing sketches of key events, role-playing characters, and developing summaries of text information.

Kathy Short, Jerome Harste, and Carolyn Burke (1996) as well as Regie Routman (2000) offer many ideas for building meaningful literature discussions.

During sustained silent reading, lovingly called DEAR (Drop Everything and Read), the teacher met with students for individual reading conferences, helped students with book selections, and monitored this quiet time to ensure that everyone had space for uninterrupted reading.

Setting learning goals and helping our students to successfully reach them means listening to their ideas, talking about areas of concern, and supporting what matters to our learners. It means connecting what goes on in our classrooms with their action plans and clearly stating how they have the responsibility for improving their learning. But it also means bringing our teaching in line with their needs and involving parents in the process so that they, too, can play a more active role in their children's education.

3

Building Progress Folios

Documenting Growth Over Time

- What Is a Progress Folio?
- How Do We Put Together a Progress Folio?
- How Do Students Show What They Know?
- How Do We Help Students Self-Evaluate?

What Is a Progress Folio?

Ten years ago, our school began keeping student writing portfolios. Teachers collected writing samples for each student at the beginning and at the end of the year. Both the student and the teacher selected these pieces. Students filled in a self-evaluation form, explaining why they chose a particular piece for their portfolio. The writing samples and self-evaluations were then filed in the students' folders and stored in a cardboard file box. At the end of the school year, the file boxes were passed on to the next grade. By the time the students reached sixth grade, their portfolios were stuffed with writing pieces, self-evaluations, and checklists for content, organization, spelling, and mechanics, marked by previous teachers. Although it was interesting to see a child's writing develop over the years, few teachers took the time to organize the work, examine the samples, use the information to plan writing lessons, or share that information with students or their parents.

If the portfolio, as a collection of student work, is not meaningful to students and never shared with parents, then it does little to improve students' learning. Portfolios should:

- "teach critical judgment as students have the opportunity to reflect and evaluate their performance" (Strickland and Strickland 2000, 92)

- "provide insights into students' self-concepts, interests, and sense of needs" (Stiggins 1997, 451)
- enable students, teachers, and parents to communicate more effectively about student progress (Hart 1994)
- enable students to become partners with teachers in the assessment process, so that they can take charge of their learning (Ames and Gahagan 1995; Hart 1994; Tierney, Carter, and Desai 1991)

Our goal is to encourage students to take responsibility for their learning, thereby promoting pride and high self-esteem. To do this, we need a system for assessment and evaluation that actively involves students, teachers, and parents, as well as a type of portfolio that facilitates this process. The *progress folio*, an extension of portfolios introduced by Colleen Politano and Anne Davies (1994, 89), helps us focus on individual student progress over time. The format for a progress folio allows student work to be organized and displayed so "the changes in key aspects of learning in reading, writing, spelling, mathematics, and the fine arts" (Politano and Davies 1994) is emphasized. Evidence of student performance is collected at several points during the school year. These examples are displayed side by side on pages that fold out, to allow for comparison of the work. Reviewing the work and reflecting on their progress, students write self-evaluations reflecting strengths, challenges and/or goals in that area. The notion of students as critical evaluators of their own performance was our goal as we developed our progress folio models.

How Do We Put Together a Progress Folio?

Our first student progress folios were large booklets made from twelve-by-eighteen-inch sheets of construction paper. Immediately we encountered problems; the construction paper tore easily when student samples were attached to it and the large size made the booklets difficult for our students to carry home to share with their families. We wanted the progress folio to be a living document of student learning, one that could be reviewed by students, teachers, or parents at any time during the year. We did not want it sitting on a shelf in the classroom.

Now we use three-ring binders for organizing student work samples. Within these binders, there are double-page formats that fold out to feature important areas of learning. Manila folders (full-cut format) are sturdy and inexpensive enough to make good pages. (See Figures 3–1 and 3–2.)

Two manila folders are needed to display each area of learning. There is room to lay four samples of student work across the two adjoining pages. We select a piece of student work from the beginning of the year to serve as a baseline sample. With this as a starting point, students can see the changes they go through as they add new pieces to their progress folio for comparison. Too often, children only see

Figure 3–1. Examples of Progress Folio Covers.

the things that are hard for them, the difficult things, and their struggles. They forget all the steps they have taken. There will always be new things for students to conquer, but we must help them take the time to recognize and celebrate the successes that have come along the way. This builds the pride and self-esteem that empower learners of all ages.

Teachers and students must work together to choose additional samples which represent their work at various points of the year. In our school, we meet with parents in November and March, so we update our progress folio at these times and use them as part of our student-led conferences (see Chapter 4). We also collect a final sample at the end of the year. With the work displayed side by side, it is easy to see the progress children make over the year.

At the beginning of the school year, children create self-portraits or some type of artwork for the progress folio covers. They also complete student information forms, webs, or "All About Me" pages for their progress folios, so that later we have another way of talking about how they began the year as a learner. (See Figures 3–3 and 3–4.) By sharing these beginning pages, everyone in the class can get to know one another. Designing their own covers and beginning with "All About Me" pages are ways children can have ownership of their folios.

What do we put into progress folios? We think about:

- What matters to the teacher?
    literacy development
    social development
    projects/content area studies

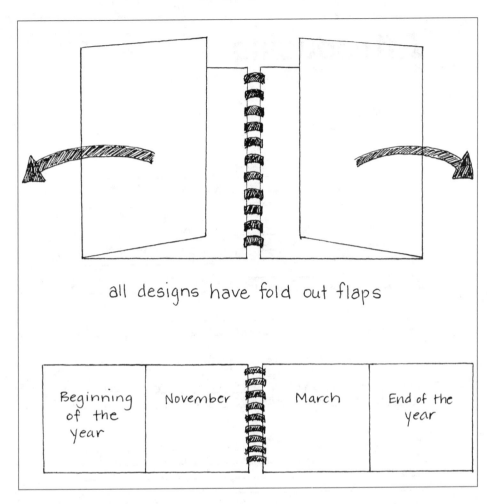

Figure 3–2A. Fold-Out Pages of Progress Folios.

Figure 3–2B. Example of Progress Folio Pages.

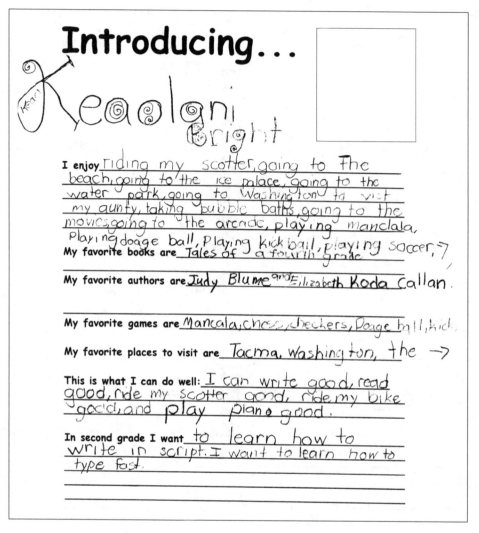

Introducing...

Keaolani Bright

I enjoy riding my scotter, going to the beach, going to the ice palace, going to the water park, going to Washington to visit my aunty, taking bubble baths, going to the movies, going to the arcade, playing manclala, Playing doage ball, Playing kick ball, playing soccer,

My favorite books are Tales of a fourth grade

My favorite authors are Judy Blume and Elizabeth Koda Callan.

My favorite games are Mancala, chess, checkers, Doage ball, kick.

My favorite places to visit are Tacma, Washington, the →

This is what I can do well: I can write good, read good, ride my scotter good, ride my bike good, and play piano good.

In second grade I want to learn how to write in script. I want to learn how to type fast.

Figure 3–3. Keaolani's All About Me Page.

- What matters to parents?
  academic growth
  social growth
- What matters to the students?
  who they are as learners
  who they are as people
  what their goals for learning are

Some teachers who use progress folios for the first time focus specifically on reading and writing progress. Other teachers feel that learning from all subject

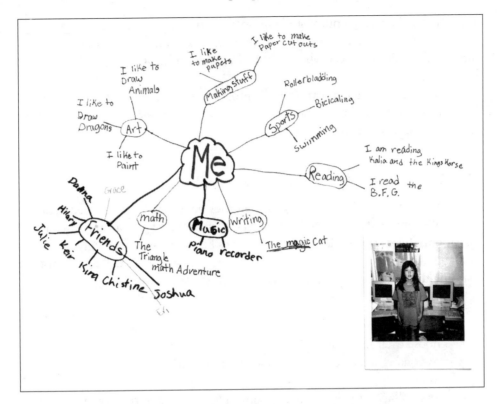

Figure 3–4. Leslie's All About Me Page.

areas should be displayed, so pages for mathematics, social studies, and science are included. Once students get the idea that these pages will be filled with evidence and examples of their learning, they also think of things they value. For example, students may wish to show what they are doing in special classes such as art, physical education, and music.

In Miki's sixth-grade classroom, the students were interested in having a memory section to glue in mementos of special events and activities. Photos, with accompanying captions, of a camp on the island of Hawai'i, hiking trips, overnight camps, and boat race day captured the unique experiences of their last year in elementary school. In Joyce's second-grade class, students asked if they could have a section for the learning they did outside of school. They talked about sports, dance lessons, piano, violin, and other hobbies and interests.

Jane Hansen (1998) talks about the importance of "valuing students' out-of-school lives," especially for students who find little success in the classroom. When we see students as *complete people*, we help them understand the complexities of life and learning. "When students share their accomplishments and struggles, they learn to value themselves and visualize a future" (Hansen

1998, 15). Older elementary students in the fifth or sixth grade are interested in adding their voice and identity to their progress folios, so sections are organized and set up to reflect what they find meaningful in their school and home lives.

Once the students construct their progress folios and decide what areas of learning are to be included, they look for evidence of their learning—what they will use to show what they know.

How Do Students Show What They Know?

Before students can select evidence of what they have learned, they need to have a good collection of items to choose from (Hansen 1998, 51). In a student-centered classroom, there are a variety of work samples because students are given choices and opportunities to decide what they will learn and how they will represent their learning. In this type of learning environment, students:

- choose their own topics for writing
- have many opportunities to write and publish their work
- choose their literature for reading
- have many opportunities for reading and sharing their ideas in literature circles
- work collaboratively in small groups to learn new information and skills
- work independently on inquiry projects and make presentations to others
- share what they have learned in a variety of ways, such as art, drama, and dance
- share what they have learned with their parents by demonstrating skills or knowledge

The process—not just the products—of learning are valued, so in addition to completed projects, research papers, and artwork, we also save drafts, revisions, notes, photographs, journals, logs, and sketches. When students share their learning with their parents, we invite the parents to tell us what they notice about their child as a reader, writer, mathematician, and learner. For example, after Mary, a second grader, took home a folktale from Sweden to share with her parents, her mother wrote back the following on the literature sharing form (see also Figure 3–5):

> Mary constantly tries. She needs to take her time as she reads. She struggled with some of the words. But she loves to read and she enjoys stories. I think it would help if she read more so she can understand more of what she reads. She did a wonderful job. She really enjoyed telling me the story.

Name *Mary*

Literature Sharing: Your child has just finished reading the book

Per and the Dala Horse

Tonight they will share the book with you and read you their favorite part. Talk with them about the story. Then complete the sections below. Thank you for participating in our literature sharing.

What I learned from the story

What a wonderful story – we have not read this book – it taught me about another country – and its folktales. I learned about each of the characters and the importance of them all. I learned about how we cherish the simple things in life. Great story.

What I thought of my child as a reader

Mary constantly tries. She needs to take her time as she reads. She struggled with some of the words. But she loves to read and she enjoys stories. I think it would help if she read more so she can understand more of what she reads. She did a wonderful job. She really enjoyed telling me the story.

Karen M.

Figure 3–5. Literature Sharing Form.

Teaching parents how they can support their child's learning by looking for strengths and needs gives them an opportunity to become active participants in the assessment and evaluation of their child. This is a new role for parents, as schools have traditionally been viewed as the experts on children and their learning. By involving parents in the assessment and evaluation process throughout the school year, and not just at reporting times, we strengthen the support for the learner by developing a partnership in learning with their parents.

To manage the accumulation of work samples that are reviewed for inclusion in progress folios, we keep all student work completed during a term in hanging file folders. These folders, one for each student, are kept in a file box in the front of the room, where they are accessible to students and teachers. When it is time to add new evidence to the progress folios, the file folders are distributed and the contents reviewed by the students. Work not selected for progress folios is then sent home.

Selecting evidence for progress folios involves teachers discussing with students what they want to show about themselves as learners and how they are progressing in school.

In one instance, Alice asked her third-grade class, "What kind of work do we put in our progress folios?" Mary said she would put in her best work, the pieces she did well on. Andy suggested putting in a sample of work that he did not do well on, so he could show what was challenging to him. Others talked about work that they had enjoyed doing because it was fun. Often, more than one piece of work was selected to show the challenges as well as accomplishments in a particular area. Listening to our students, it is clear that they have many ideas about which work samples should go in their progress folios, including pieces that show

- their best work
- something they are not doing well and need help with
- a strength or talent they have
- what they are learning
- growth or improvement
- the many different kinds of things that they do in school
- what they are interested in and enjoy

Good readers and good writers charts, started early in the year, are used to help students select their evidence. One day in November, at the end of the first term, students in JoAnn's second-grade class were adding evidence to the reading section of their progress folios.

"What have we been doing as readers?" asked JoAnn.

"We have been reading lots of books," said Karen.

"How do we show that?" asked JoAnn.

"We have our reading logs to show what we read each month," suggested Mary.

"What else have we done in reading?"

"We finished our study of *Stone Fox* and have our literature journals," said Jack.

"We also read our current events articles in *Time for Kids*. It's not a story, but we do have to read for information," commented Kyle.

"So if we look at our good readers chart, have we been working to improve ourselves as readers since September?" asked JoAnn.

Looking up at the chart, Stephanie raised her hand. "It says, *good readers read a variety of books*. My reading log shows all the books that I've been reading."

"Good connection, Stephanie."

"I am reading more chapter books now," Stephanie added.

"When we look at our literature log for *Stone Fox*, what does that show about us as readers?"

"We are learning to write down our ideas about the books we read," said Mark.

"You certainly are, and that's another thing we said good readers do, they *understand what they read*," JoAnn replied.

As the students reviewed the work they were doing as readers, JoAnn made a listing of these ideas on the board. "Today we are looking for evidence of what we have done as readers this term. Take a look at your folders, and select those pieces that you want to add to your progress folios."

Then the work folders were passed out and students began sorting through the various pieces saved since September, selecting a range of work to show who they were as readers. The selected pieces were added to their progress folios, and items not chosen were sent home.

After selecting appropriate evidence of learning, such as in the above example, students need time to reflect and critically evaluate their progress by looking at what they have achieved and the difficulties they faced. There may be confusion when we use the terms *self-reflect*, *self-evaluate*, and *self-assess*. All are important to consider as we encourage students to look over their growth and learning, but each term asks a slightly different question (Hill and Ruptic 1994, 164):

Self-Reflection: What did I learn? How do I feel about my learning?
Self-Evaluation: How did I do? How have I improved? What are my strengths? What are my areas for growth?
Self-Assessment: How do I learn best? How am I growing? What is still unclear? What is getting easier?

Typically, students write what they think teachers want, but find little value or meaning in the task. We want students to reflect on their learning not just for us, but for their *own* purposes, so they can value their learning, value themselves as learners, and move forward in their learning. To do this, we need to provide students with opportunities for meaningful reflection, guidance and modeling of self-evaluation, and acceptance of their values, goals, and ideas.

How Do We Help Students Self-Evaluate?

Throughout the year, we give our students opportunities to take responsibility for their own learning. We identify their responsibilities as learners and support them as they take on greater responsibilities, setting goals and assessing their progress:

> If we focus on the student as one of the essential evaluators in the portfolio process, then we place ourselves in a teaching/learning role. Students cannot handle this step without sound teaching and demonstration by the teacher. (Graves and Sunstein 1992, 3)

Evaluating their own learning is a struggle for many primary students. They are seldom asked to write about their learning, or if they are given the opportunity they are not able to make thoughtful judgments. Just as often, teachers recognize the importance of students evaluating their own learning, but do not know effective ways to accomplish this. Teachers may set up checklists, questionnaires, conduct interest or attitude surveys, and have students create self-portraits.

We are careful not to rely on these forms as our sole source of student evaluation; we incorporate other forms of student self-evaluation throughout the year. For example, after students select the samples they want to include in their progress folio, they complete self-evaluation forms and attach them to the pieces. For grades 2 and above, we prefer using more open-ended formats that allow students to write on their own. They note what has been easy or difficult a that particular area, and explain key features of selected work samples (see Figure 3–6). This is often done with the teacher's help at the beginning of the year, but becomes an independent activity as the children have more practice with self-evaluation.

In some first-grade classrooms, reading and writing checklists are helpful. Teachers often meet with children individually to review these checklists with them as they look at work samples (see Figure 3–7).

In other classrooms teachers may use some type of prompts to help children articulate their ideas. These prompts provide meaningful contexts for thinking about progress, and children can fill in the missing parts of the text (see Figure 3–8).

Date: ___12/14___

This is an example of . . .

___Writing Work___

I want you to notice that . . .

my island story was hard to think of because I had
change alot of things. This year I have tried to
make paragraf's on my writing. I have good Ideas
and I am curious and I like the biography's I wrote
about a teacher and my brother.

Figure 3–6. Self-Evaluation Form.

We realize, however, that in order for students to articulate their ideas clearly and to find this type of evaluation meaningful, reflection and self-evaluation have to be a part of our everyday classroom routines, and not just something we do two or three times a year. Following are some successful ways we have found to support meaningful self-reflection and self-evaluation throughout the year.

Informal Self-Evaluations

Informal reflection can be simple and quick. Students might assess progress on an assignment with a thumbs up or thumbs down signal, or assess their progress or participation on a project with a happy or sad face. After a writing workshop, for example, Joyce stopped to ask her second graders what they found hard about the writing that day, and what they found easy. This was one informal way she brought self-evaluation into her daily routine.

Formal Self-Evaluations

Older students benefit from formal reflections on learning and progress after major units of study—book reflections after a literature study, writing reflections after completing a published piece, learning reflections after completing a project. Joyce has her second-grade students complete project evaluation forms, which gives

Middle of the Year Self-evaluation

I like to write. (Yes) No

As a writer, I ...

✓write about many different kinds of things

"Sometimes"leave spaces between my words

" unless I can't fit it"use capital letters at the beginning of a sentence

✓use periods

__use question marks

✓use exclamation points

✓use what I know to help me spell words

" I try to "write sentences that make sense

To improve my writing I will

"figure out more words."

_____

Figure 3-7A. Middle of the Year Self-Evaluation.

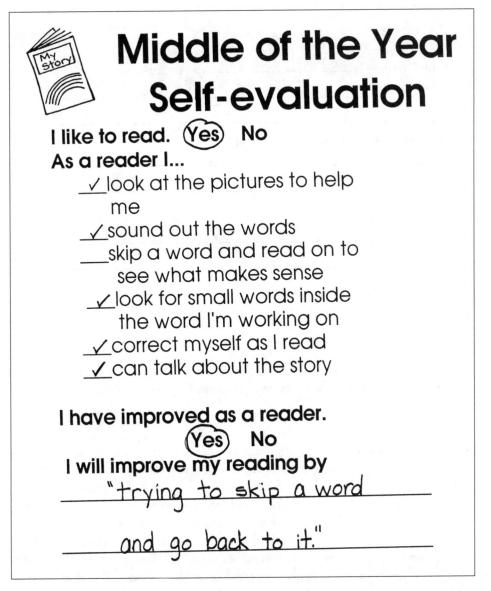

Middle of the Year Self-evaluation

I like to read. (Yes) No

As a reader I...

✓ look at the pictures to help me

✓ sound out the words

___ skip a word and read on to see what makes sense

✓ look for small words inside the word I'm working on

✓ correct myself as I read

✓ can talk about the story

I have improved as a reader.
(Yes) No

I will improve my reading by

"trying to skip a word

and go back to it."

Figure 3-7B. Middle of the Year Self-Evaluation.

As a writer,

I think writing is ___*fun*___ because
___*you can get ideas qikle*___

_____

As a writer I can do these things well,
___*foces / think / do my work*___

_____

I can improve as a writer by,
___*putting meaning and feeling in my*___
___*writing*___

Figure 3-8. Writing Self-Evaluation Form.

them experience with rating their work based on class- or teacher-determined criteria. (See Figure 3–9 for a sample evaluation.)

Weekly Progress Sheet

Both Alice and Joyce use weekly progress sheets in their classrooms. Students write down their daily assignments, and spend a few minutes at the end of each day writing a reflection of their learning (see Figure 3–10). The reflection is often goal-related or simply something they would like to comment on—something they enjoyed, learned, or did well that day. In addition, Alice and Joyce add their own comments to the progress sheets, which are often sent home along with samples of work completed during the week. Parents are invited to share their thoughts on the appropriate space on the progress sheet and return it to school. The work samples and progress sheets are then kept in the work folders as evidence of learning.

Learning to reflect and evaluate takes time, patience, and practice, especially at the beginning of the school year. Students are learning new skills and the language of assessment and evaluation. But as students continue to repeat the cycle of selecting evidence and reflecting on progress, they develop the ability to communicate their learning. They become more independent and begin to see how the cycle helps them improve as learners. This is especially evident when we compare

NAME _____

DATE _____

NATIVE AMERICAN PROJECT EVALUATION

4–5 EXCELLENT, SUPER, WOW!

  Work and information were accurate.

  Used a good number of materials; work was not skimpy.

  Illustrations or display was thorough, colorful, neat.

  Work was neat, carefully done.

  Included a title of tribe.

  Project was eye-catching.

  Super effort!

3 VERY GOOD—GOOD SHOW!

  Work and information were accurate.

  Had at least 3–4 of the above items.

  Good effort shown.

2 OK—SATISFACTORY

  Could have been neater.

  Lacked information, or display was skimpy.

  Some effort.

1 Not much effort.

  Not much thought put into it.

Your evaluation: I thought I deserved a _____ rating because

_____

_____

Classmate's evaluation: I thought you deserved a _____ rating

because _____

_____

I liked _____

Mrs. Ahuna's evaluation: I thought you deserved a _____ rating because

_____

_____

Figure 3-9. Project Evaluation Form.

Weekly Progress

Name: TROY
Date: 3/13

My goal for the week is _to write good reflection for my progress folio work_

Monday 3/13/00 Assignments & Events	Feelings	Daily Reflection
Progross folio	😊 😐	On Progress folio's I improved because I wrote one page and now I wrote three pages. I am on my second reflection paper. I'm felling exellent.
Rehersal		
Progress folio		
P.E.		
MAth		
reflection		
sharing China postcards		

Tuesday 3/14/00 Assignments & Events	Feelings	Daily Reflection
Progress folio	😄	I finished my Progress folio this is an example of ... I made a cool tie in Art. I felt exited when I found a good book in the Library. I felt nurvus because I didn't finish my progress folio then I finished it.
Art make-up		
Library		
reflection		
Share China postcards		

Wednesday 3/15/00 Assignments & Events	Feelings	Daily Reflection
Progress folios		My ultimate seat was my usual seat. I finished my progress folio. At art I felt nervous because I almost didn't finish my thing then I did. 😊
Art		
reflection		
share China postcard		

Figure 3-10. Completed Weekly Progress Chart.

Thursday 3/16/00 Assignments & Events	Feelings	Daily Reflection
China folk scrolls		On my china folk scroll I
P.E.		felt exellent because I thought
sharing postcards		mine was good. Sharing
reflection		China postcards was fun to
share china postcards		tell the other kids about
		China.

Friday 3/17/00 Assignments & Events		Daily Reflection
Chapel		I had a sub which was Mrs. Yee because we had confrences.
spelling test		At chapel it showed god
scrolls		making the world. I made
Music share		a good scroll. We had
Mrs. Ogata china postcard		music in chapel because
		we did a rehersal.

How did I do this week?

student I had a good time because I finished my scroll.

teacher Wow! Your scrolls show many details. I love the Chinese temples. They look like the Japanese pagodas. I can't wait to see them after they are painted!

parent comment

I see much improvement in Troy's expressive writing — keep up the great work! I'm looking forward to seeing your postcard! — Peggy Jaylor

Figure 3-10. (continued)

self-evaluation comments from beginning to end. The number of comments increases, the comments become more specific, and students show more insight into their needs as learners.

Our students are learning much more than can ever be measured quantitatively. How do we know this? We take the time to ask them what they think of their progress folios and the time we have spent looking at ourselves as learners. Here's what they shared with us:

- I enjoyed my progress folio because it gave me a chance to express things I enjoy. It will help me to show progress every term because I can go back and look on my other terms and reach a higher goal, more toward the independent side.
- My progress folio helps me to see what I have done in that term. It helps me to be an independent learner because you can see all the evidence you have and how you can accomplish your goals.
- When my parents looked inside my mom was so proud of me. It helps me to see where I am at and where I have to go.
- I enjoyed the progress folio because I got to choose pieces that show how I improved in my work. It helped my parents understand my progress because throughout the year I added to it and they saw how my work improved.
- My progress folio taught me a lot of things. I also thought that it was cool because I got to say things about me and got to choose my own things.
- My progress folio was very fun and it made me work very hard. It helped me to be an independent learner because I had to look at all my things I have to improve on.
- I like the progress folio better than grades because it shows evidence of what I did.

We guide our students toward becoming active participants and evaluators of their own learning. Our classrooms support student choice, goalsetting, and action plans. We create documents—progress folios—that provide evidence of our progress, and we share them with parents as well as teachers and classmates. The next step is the formal sharing of our progress folios at student-led conferences. This conference is important because it "is the primary opportunity for the vital discussion and review of ideas that are the heart of the portfolio process . . . these conferences . . . help ensure that the portfolio is more than a kind of unique file folder—more than a mere place to store samples of student's work" (Farr and Tone 1994, 134).

4

Bridging Learning, Assessing, and Reporting Through Student-Led Conferences

- Why Use Student-Led Conferences?
- How Do We Prepare for a Successful Conference?
- How Do We Prepare Parents for a Student-Led Conference?

Josh and his mother sit side by side at a round table with his teacher sitting across from them. Josh begins the conference by sharing his progress folio. He opens to the first section, reading, and reads aloud his self-evaluation. Then he shows his mother the attached written response to literature and reading log. Josh starts out nervously, but as he speaks his confidence blossoms. His voice becomes stronger and he slows his pace. He reads his evaluations, then adds his own spontaneous comments: "See, this is the book I brought home to practice reading with expression." His mother gives nods of approval and a warm smile.

Josh moves from the reading section to the writing section and shows his mother the rough draft of his dolphin story. He reads his evaluation about this piece and shares how he uses *golden nuggets* in his story.

His mother asks, "What are golden nuggets?"

"It's when you use words to paint pictures in the reader's head," replies Josh. He points out "the glazing, shimmering water" section in his story as an example. Josh gets up from the table to retrieve the completed dolphin story from his desk. He proudly shows his mother how he has started to publish his story.

Josh is taking an active role in reporting his learning to his parents. In addition to showing his own progress, he teaches his parents what it takes to be a good reader and writer. His teacher is there to support him and assist as needed, but Josh finds the courage and confidence to complete the sharing on his own.

Why Use Student-Led Conferences?

Reporting student progress to parents has traditionally been the teacher's responsibility. It is consistent with the belief that teachers are the *givers of knowledge* and students are simply *empty vessels* to be filled. Parents often take a passive role in parent-teacher conferences, listening and asking few questions, relying instead on the teacher—the expert—for a full report on their child. The students are not invited to participate in the conferences. They too, rely on the teacher to speak for them.

As we shift to the constructivist view of learning, where children *actively build* their own understanding of the world around them, then we have to acknowledge that they are also constructing their own understanding of themselves and their learning. Therefore, in addition to determining goals, making action plans, and evaluating their own progress based on critical review of their performance, students need to take responsibility for participating in parent-teacher conferences. These conferences are often called *student-led conferences.*

Much has been written in the last few years describing the benefits of students discussing their progress with their parents. Richard Stiggins (1997, 499) reports that when students are involved in their conferences, they have

- a stronger sense of responsibility for their own learning,
- a stronger sense of pride,
- a more productive relationship with their teachers, and
- improved relationships with their parents.

In addition, student-led conferences

- build a stronger sense of community in the classroom,
- develop leadership skills in children, and
- support greater parental participation in conferences.

Regie Routman also points out that "the biggest advantage of student-led conferences . . . is that parents understand what their child is learning because the child can explain it, supported by the portfolio" (2000, 579).

A student-led conference typically begins with students greeting their parents, grandparents, or guardians and thanking them for taking the time to come to the conference. As in Josh's conference, the student sits beside his parents with his conference planning guide and progress folio. The student starts the conference, but the teacher is always there for support, to clarify things when needed, and to answer questions. The teacher also models for parents how to respond to what the child is sharing. Parents are encouraged to ask questions at any time. When goals are discussed, the student shares what he will do to work on his goals, and the teacher shares how she will support him and solicits parent help.

Let's return to Josh's conference. After he shares his progress folio, Josh reads from his conference planning guide, which he filled out earlier in class. Using the guide, he identifies his strengths, challenges, and goals.

Strengths

- Reads with more expression.
- Does homework and reads nightly.
- Did well on Continental Math League problems.
- Remembers to do his class job.
- Problem-solving skills have improved.

Challenges

- Read different types of books.
- Find topics to write about.
- Don't rush when doing assignments.

Goals

- Read different types of books.
- Complete assignments neatly.

Josh's teacher says that that she will help him find different books to read, and she will remind him about the class chart that lists the criteria for completed work. The teacher then turns to Josh's mother and asks her how she could support Josh's goals at home. His mother says that they can go to the library more often to get books. She also said she would remind him to complete his homework neatly, and make sure he has enough time to do so.

In this classroom, we see how Josh led his conference by explaining his work samples to his mother. He then mentioned how he was able to achieve his goals, and answered his mother's question about golden nuggets. As Josh shared his work, his teacher was in the background, listening and not interrupting. Both Josh's mother and teacher stated how they would support him in working toward his goals. The tone of the conference was one of *celebrating* Josh's accomplishments and *supporting* his learning.

Teachers observe positive changes from parents after these student-led conferences:

- Parents have a better understanding of the curriculum and strategies used in the classroom.

- Parents show an interest in playing a more active role in their child's education by taking them to the library, reading with them at night, going over writing and other assignments, and giving one-on-one help with goals.
- Parents work more collaboratively with the teacher and their child.
- Parents have an optimistic attitude about school.

Many parents of students at different grade levels echo support for student-led conferences. Following are comments from parents about these conferences.

Mr. Kinau, Sixth-Grade Parent

I believe it is positive to have Michelle critically assess her progress and to take responsibility for her own learning. It also provides me with further insight into what is important and meaningful to her with regard to her studies.

Mrs. Holt, Second-Grade Parent

Communication is very important. Conferences with progress folios allow us to see as well as hear how much my daughter has progressed. I am more and more impressed each time. Jessie has come a long way in writing. We shared her stories with our whole family and they enjoyed every bit!

Mrs. Adams, Fifth-Grade Parent

I liked having Vance show me his accomplishments. I know that Vance knows where he stands as far as his strengths and weaknesses, and where he needs to improve.

Mr. Paulson, Third-Grade Parent

We like it when Lisa is sitting in. This way we don't have to go home and discuss the conference with her. We found it to be very informative. Setting goals gives the students an idea of what to strive for.

Mrs. Alama, Second-Grade Parent

As a second grader, when Kacey shared her progress folio for the first time, she was really scared because she had never been invited to a parent conference before. I know that if I went to a parent-teacher conference with my mom, I would think that the teacher would only have something bad to say something I couldn't do, or that I was junk in this. She was afraid that perhaps the teacher would talk about something that came up in school. So she was pretty nervous knowing that she was going to be right there, and mom and dad were going to be sitting with the teacher. But talking about the progress folio together in the conference made her understand why parents want to meet with teachers. It's not for the teacher to complain. It made her understand why teachers work with parents. Our conference was really good.

We receive many supportive comments from parents and see changes in our children after student-led conferences. Students are more focused in their work, and there is more enthusiasm and a genuine sense of pride in themselves and what they accomplish. They ask for help to work on weak areas not just from teachers but from classmates as well. For example, one of Mary's goals was to find books by different authors to read. She had many books by Dick King-Smith on her reading log, but few others. The next time the class went to the library, her friend Kathy showed her books she had read by Ruth Chew, and another friend, Megan, located some Roald Dahl books for her.

We have been conducting student-led conferences for several years, and we continue to marvel at how students and parents successfully work together to support improvements in learning. Student-led conferences are an important aspect of student-centered learning and evaluation.

How Do We Prepare for a Successful Conference?

Student-led conferences can be difficult because they

- take a lot of time,
- take planning and hard work by students and teachers,
- mean clearly communicating ideas,
- mean encouraging parent participation, and
- mean helping students so they succeed. (Routman 2000; Stiggins 1997)

While we faced challenges implementing student-led conferences, we found ways to streamline the process so it became part of our ongoing assessment and evaluation system. Starting with Davies, Politano, Cameron, and Gregory's (1992) plans for three-way conferencing, we looked at what would work with our students and the time constraints we had for conferences, and identified three important things that help us prepare for student-led conferences. They were:

- conference planning guides
- student-teacher conferences
- conference role-playing

We allowed two weeks for progress folio preparation. During our reading workshop, we would spend forty-five minutes to an hour reviewing goals and looking over completed work. Part of that time was spent selecting evidence and writing self-evaluations. On another day we allotted the same amount of time during writing workshop for selecting writing evidence. As students became familiar with the process of reviewing, reflecting, and evaluating, they moved through the math, social studies, and science sections much quicker. Later in the year, less teacher support was needed, but thirty to forty-five minutes was still scheduled for this process.

Conference Planning Guides

Once the students update their progress folios, they need time to look them over to decide what is important to share with their parents. In the short time allowed for conferences—thirty minutes or less—students cannot cover every item in their progress folios. With the help of conference planning guides, students can identify main areas they need to discuss with parents to enlist their support, and what evidence they want to show. Using a conference planning guide helps to alleviate some of the anxiety inherent at conferences. With younger students, a teacher might choose to interview them before the conference and ask them to share two things they did well and one thing they still need to work on. The teacher can then jot notes down on a conference planning form for them (see Figure 4–1).

Another form our students have used successfully is "My Informal Report to My Parents" (see Figure 4–2). We adapted this guide from one created by Anne Davies, Caren Cameron, Colleen Politano, and Kathleen Gregory (1992). As they complete this form, students share more about their learning by identifying key areas of progress and challenge and citing reasons for success or difficulty. Students in grades 2 and above can usually complete this form on their own.

We use a conference planning guide to prepare our own information for conferences (see Figure 4–3). Similar to the form used by students, ours has room to note our observations of student progress. We use information from our anecdotal notes, grade books, checklists, and our own review of the progress folio. When meeting with twenty-five or more students, this conference planning guide keeps us organized and focused.

Giving students the time to prepare what they want to share beforehand helps them feel more confident about talking with their parents; they know what they are going to say and what they will show from their progress folios to support their comments. Taking the time to prepare a conference planning guide ourselves allows us to focus on each student. The next step is for the student and teacher to sit down together and review the conference plan.

Student-Teacher Conferences

Christine, a second grader, brings her conference planning guide and her progress folio to her teacher, JoAnn. JoAnn also has a conference planning guide, on which she has noted ideas for the student-led conference. During the

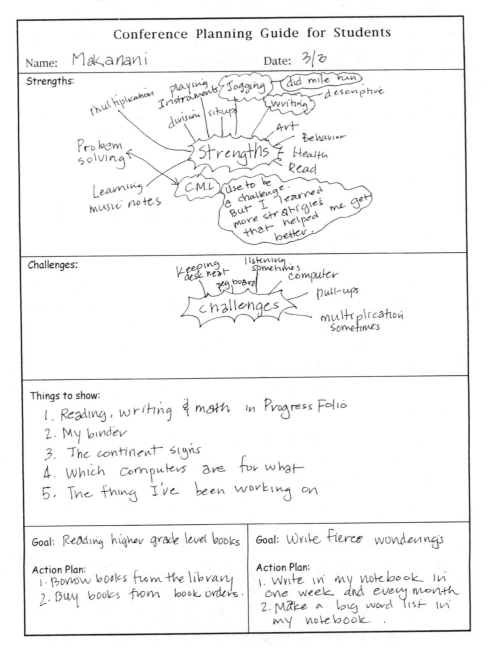

Figure 4–1. Conference Planning Guide for Students.

My Informal Report to My Parents
Grade 1   D3

Name: Date: 3/15

1. The most important thing in our classroom that I am trying to do well is
   being responsible and independent. I'm also trying
   to be a better speller too.

2. This is important to me because
   when I'm responsible and independent I'll be abel to learn
   better.

3. Two things I have done well this past month are
   reading because I can read some hard capter books in about
   two weeks. I think I'm doing good in writeing because I'm
   geting my writeing work done.

4. One thing that I need to work harder at is
   Spelling because some big words are hard for me.

5. My goal(s) for the next month is (are) geting better at spelling. And
   madminutes is challenging for me because some times it's
   hard for me to answer the prodlem.

6. I'd like to share some of my work with you. Please notice that
   I'm geting more independent and more responsible.

Figure 4–2. Student's Informal Report to Parents.

Conference Guide for Teachers

Name: Jennifer   Date: 11/04

Strengths:	Challenges:

reading:
  applies strategies taught
  reads daily
writing / behavior
  persistent, keeps at her work
  uses resources to help her
    write
behavior –
  listens   Sits in the front
  follows directions good attitude
  focuses
  tries to participate
	reading:
	  fluency
	  decoding words
	writing
	  fluency – putting ideas down
	  spelling words
	(Jan) – improved
	* beginning reading w/ her each
	  day.

Notes for the conference: fall - importance of reading daily - IRI P- reading level	Notes for the conference: spring
Goal(s) and Action Plans for fall Read daily 1. log reading 2. read with mom, dad or brother Learning new words 1. write them in personal dictionary 2. share with family + teacher	Goal(s) and Action Plans for spring

Student will . . .
  read to parents at home and
  T. in school during recess, reading or
                       dear.
Teacher will . . .
  listen to J. read each day.
  log book, note progress
Parent will . . .
  support J. at home. Read
  daily with her.
	Student will . . .
	
	Teacher will . . .
	
	Parent will . . .

Figure 4–3. Conference Guide for Teachers.

student-teacher conference, JoAnn will listen to find out what ideas Christine has about her progress, and compare them to her own notes. This helps to ensure that important points of concern are not overlooked.

Christine begins by reading, "The most important thing that I am trying to do well is my writing. This is important to me because I don't know what to write about."

"Christine, that's a good point you brought up about your writing. I have that same idea on my notes. What do you have to show that this is hard?" asks JoAnn.

"I can show these pages from my writing notebook." Christine opens her progress folio to show pages that she has taken from her composition book and put into the second quarter section of her progress folio. These pages show two or three sentences where she has started ideas about going fishing with her dad or describing flowers in her garden. Christine has started to choose her own topics for writing, but continues to need help developing them: "I'll show them that I can think of ideas, but I'm still having a hard time knowing what to write next."

Confident that Christine will be able to explain her writing needs to her parents, JoAnn has Christine continue to read from her conference plan. "Two things I am proud of are my reading and my math. I was able to do well because I spend a lot of time reading and I like math."

Again, JoAnn asks Christine to tell her more about her reading and math, since she has noted these as areas of Christine's strengths on her own conference planning sheet.

"I spend at least an hour reading every night," Christine says. "See, here on my reading log I have many books listed. Some took me a long time because they were chapter books. But I love to read. I get stuck in books and can't stop. I want to show my math problem-solving papers because I have gotten better at drawing pictures to help figure out the answer. They used to be hard problems, but now I can do it by myself."

"Great, Christine. I can see you will have a lot to share with your parents," congratulates JoAnn.

This is just one example of a student-teacher conference where students are asked to present their agenda for the conference and how they will show their parents their strengths and challenges. Learning to articulate their ideas and reasoning is difficult at first, and students need guidance from their teacher. It is at the student-teacher conference that this support is provided. In this one-on-one situation, teachers ask questions to promote students' thinking and praise efforts at sharing their learning. To have students think more about their learning, teachers can ask:

- How did you know that was hard?
- What can you use to show that?
- What made it easier for you?
- What does that show about you as a reader? A writer? A mathematician? A learner?
- How have you changed?
- What can we do to help you?

Teachers can also praise their efforts with specific comments, such as:

- You really know yourself well.
- You were honest about what has been hard.
- You have a good goal.
- You have chosen good evidence to show what you have done well.
- You have good evidence for what has been challenging.

When we began holding student-teacher conferences, it was difficult listening to students talk about their work and what they noticed about themselves as learners—without interrupting them. We were used to telling the students what they were good at and what they needed to do better, because that was the traditional role assigned to us. Now, we listen, ask questions, and share what we have noticed. It is a collaborative discussion, where we honor what has been done well and seek direction for further growth and improvement.

At the beginning of the year, twenty minutes per student was needed to adequately prepare them for their conferences. This time was squeezed into silent reading time, independent work periods, recess, and before or after school hours. It took about a week to meet with twenty-five students. Later in the year, as teachers and students knew their goals and needs better, conferences were shortened to ten or fifteen minutes. While these conferences do take a great deal of time, teachers admit that this is where they learn the most about their students.

Conference Role-Playing

In situations where students will be participating in a student-led conference for the first time, it is helpful to role-play the situation. Students can form small groups of three or four and take turns portraying parents and teachers. Those playing students can use their conference planning sheets and progress folios to share their learning, and those playing parents can ask questions. It is wise to remind students that this is to help them be better prepared for their own conference, so they should be respectful of each other's sharing. It is amazing how the classroom community pulls together at this time. They are aware of each other's goals and have been helping to support them. They sometimes remind their classmates of other things they have done to work toward their goals that both the teacher and student have forgotten. During these role-playing situations, teachers listen in on the conversations to help those students having trouble knowing what to do next or to compliment groups that are working well together.

Teachers should model the conference first, so students can visualize and hear what is expected of them. The following example shows a demonstration that Joyce gave to her class.

Joyce sat next to Kristin, with Kristin's progress folio in front of them. They faced the class, and Joyce told them that she was going to pretend to be Kristin and Kristin would pretend to be her mother. Joyce began by saying, "Mom, this is my progress folio and I'm going to show you what I've learned this quarter." She opened the progress folio, explained the introduction sheet, and proceeded to the first section, which was reading. "This quarter I wanted to work on reading fluently and smoothly. I set this as my reading goal," said Joyce. She showed a couple of pages from the book *Big Al* and read the pages with confidence and fluency, while Kristin listened.

Joyce then asked Kristin and the rest of the class, "What do you think her parents might ask or say?"

Kristin responded in an adult voice, "Very good. You read smoothly." The class howled at Kristin's portrayal of her mom.

From this skit, the class came up with criteria for a successful conference:

- Make sure your progress folio is complete.
- Practice for your conference.
- Be calm; don't be nervous.
- Don't rush; explain thoroughly.
- Speak in a loud, clear voice.
- Be serious.
- Be sure to read your self-evaluations.
- After you have shared, ask your parents if they have questions or comments.

We want student-led conferences to be as successful as possible and we take as many steps as needed to prepare our students for this event.

How Do We Prepare Parents for a Student-Led Conference?

We begin working with parents long before student-led conferences are held. Parents are used to the traditional method of reporting progress—report cards and parent-teacher conferences—and haven't been given the opportunity to take a more active role in assessment and evaluation with their children. They, too, need to develop new skills. We found five effective ways of working with our parents:

- open house sharing
- homework with parents
- informal reporting or progress checks
- class newsletters
- learning nights or in-school sharing

Open House Sharing

Every school has some time set aside at the beginning of the year where parents are invited to school to meet their child's teacher and learn more about expectations for the year. At this time, we share the early stages of our progress folio—student information pages and perhaps baseline samples. We tell parents how, through the year, we will document their child's growth with self-evaluations and work samples as evidence. We have on hand a completed example of a progress folio to show what the end product will look like.

We also ask parents to write us a letter telling us about their child from their perspective. We gain a deeper understanding and appreciation for children when we see them through their parents' eyes. Figures 4–4 and 4–5 show examples of two letters we use.

At this time, we also introduce student-led conferences, in which their child will play an important role. We assure parents that there will be time available after the student-led conference to discuss any private matters of concern. Preparing parents for discussing their child's progress with their child present begins at open house and continues throughout the term until the actual conference.

Homework with Parents

After students learn a new mathematics strategy or game, perform an interesting science experiment, or complete a literature study on a particular book, we ask them to share this learning with their parents as homework. By playing the role of the teacher, and showing their parents what they know, students actively demonstrate their newly acquired skills and knowledge. As part of the homework assignment, parents are often asked to respond in writing to let us know what they learned from the activity and what they noticed about their child. These activities emphasize the wonderful things their child is learning to do, rather than what they can't do.

August 24, 2001

Dear Parents,

Please take a few minutes to complete this form and return it to school by Friday, September 1st. The information you share will help me assess your child's strengths and challenges. This feedback will also communicate your concerns and expectations you have for your child.

Mahalo,

A. Kimura

I feel that my child . . . is excited for this school year. She loves school and all of the new things she learns. She tends to be a bit tender and is very caring. She is a sweet girl with an air of innocents. I hope you enjoy her as much as I know she will enjoy you. She loves learning and is eager to read better and better! (◡)

I worry that my child . . . has an enjoyable art experience. For some reason, she tends to get "worked up" over art. She often cries the night before and is very anxious about it. I have tried very hard to encourage her and inform her that art is supposed to be fun. Her last year's teacher talked with the art teacher and she was surprised. So, I worry about her and hope that she can overcome whatever it is about art. Keep me informed.

I hope that my child . . . has a super 1st grade year and is happy. She loves school and I simply want that love of learning to continue. I hope she makes new friends and has a great year! (◡)

Child's name: Donna Collins

Parent Signature: Denise Collins

Figure 4–4. Parent Letter.

Dear Parents,

Welcome to the start of another school year. Thank you for sharing your child with me for this short time in their journey through life. I would like to become a partner with you in your child's education, so I can make a contribution that lasts a lifetime.

My teaching begins with your child, having them feel at home in my classroom, and helping all children to come together as a community of learners. Would you help me by taking a moment to write me about your child? What is your child like? What are things that you feel are important for me to know? What are your child's interests? I want to get to know how your child as a learner and as a person.

This is our first step toward building a successful partnership in learning between student, parent, and teacher.

Mahalo,
JoAnn Wong-Kam

Figure 4–5. Parent Letter About Child.

Informal Reporting or Progress Checks

Prior to conferences, about midway in a reporting period, students look at their work folders, select a few pieces, and briefly evaluate their progress on an informal evaluation form (see Appendix C, Figure C-8). The samples are chosen to represent a variety of areas of study, including reading, writing, mathematics, and content areas.

In addition to student evaluations, teachers write cover letters explaining the work that is being sent home, the goals of the assignments, the expectations for the quality of the work at that time, and the areas that the class is working to improve. The students go over the work samples with their parents, telling what they learned and sharing their self-evaluations. Parents are asked to write a short response to their child about the sharing. In first grade we ask that they start with two positive comments—stars—then select one wish, something they would like their child to work on next. (See Appendix C, Figure C-9.)

In other classrooms, in addition to providing spaces for compliments and suggestions for future work, feedback forms give parents the opportunity to write a comment or question to the teacher (see Figure 4–6). The parents' responses are shared with the students and also serve as valuable feedback for the teacher on parent concerns prior to the conference. The positive tone of the feedback sheet models for parents what is important to us at this time, in order to help their child. We need to highlight children's strengths and what they have done well, as well as consider the areas they need more help with.

Dear Parents,

Your child is bringing home work recently done in class. Your child has written a self-evaluation about this work, sharing what he/she has been trying to do well, two things he/she is proud of, and identifying something he/she would like help with.

   Please take a few quiet minutes to listen and learn as your child shares work samples with you. Celebrate areas of achievement and offer encouragement on the things your child finds challenging.

   We are asking that you add your comments about your child's learning on the form below, and return the form and the work samples to school by_____.

   Thank you for working with us to bring success to your child's learning.

. . . .

Dear ___Amy___,

   After looking at your work, we would like to compliment you on
your beautiful story. You gave me a really nice feeling for
Running Deer and her family, and what her life was like. We
are happy that you enjoy school. We are very proud of your
reading, writing, and math skills. I am especially proud that
you concentrated on your goal of focusing and active listening
and now you don't need so many reminders. Hooray!
   We would like to support you as you continue to work on

organizing your thoughts better, being neater and
improving your penmanship.

                              Mr. and Mrs. Lum

_____

   Comments or questions for the teacher

Thank you for working with Amy to bring out her
best qualities. She loves school and learning about
new things. Thank you for keeping her on-task
and for keeping us informed on how she is doing.

Figure 4–6. Parent Comment.

Class Newsletters

Maintaining open communication with parents is an important step in order to focus student-led conferences on supporting student learning. Too often, parents come with concerns that could have been addressed earlier if there were an ongoing system of communication between home and school. Classroom newsletters have helped us to fill that need (see Figure 4–7). Whether you have a monthly or weekly newsletter, parents benefit from:

- knowing the curriculum focus at that time,
- noting important dates for upcoming events,
- being informed of the expectations for work,
- seeing examples of student work,
- gaining information about curriculum, and
- reading about things they can do at home to help their child.

When parents understand expectations, see examples of student work, and are given information on how they can help their child, they become active members of the learning team. Student-led conferences also serve to give parents feedback on how they can further improve learning for their child.

Learning Nights or In-School Sharing

In our school we occasionally sponsor learning nights, where we open our classrooms and share activities with parents to show them how we are working with their children in different areas of the curriculum. Learning nights are often held in conjunction with PTA events. In our school, we have had learning nights that focused on mathematics, reading, and writing, as well as music and Hawaiian language and culture. Parents come away with a much clearer understanding of what their children do while they are at school and can offer more support because they now see the *process* and not just the *product*.

At other times we have in-school events where students hold demonstrations of their learning for their parents. In one school, students plan a Grandparents Day. Grandparents come to see their children sing and present poems or stories, then visit classrooms to see the work they have done (see Figure 4–8). Students often act as guides through the art and writing sample displays. In another school, third graders put on a multicultural evening with exhibits, interactive display, models, and food samples from different cultures around the world. Again, students are the guides and provide information to their parents and family members about what they have learned.

In whatever form sharing takes place, the more parents get to experience and see, the better they will be able to participate in student-led conferences because they have a bigger picture of all the learning that goes on with their child.

Ke Anuenue o Punahou.

http://www.punahou.edu/js/grade2/f2/index.html

January 19, 2001
Punahou School   Grade 2   F-2

Hawaii's Plantation Village

We had a great time at Waipahu Cultural Garden visiting the Arakawa Museum and the homes of the people who came to work on the sugar plantations. Read more about this exciting field trip in next week's newsletter.

Robinson Crusoe

This week the children have been reliving the adventures of a shipwrecked sailor named Robinson Crusoe. Sometimes I will read a chapter aloud to the class and share the images and ideas the get from the passages. Modeling what good readers do is an important step in helping the children become critical thinkers. Then students get together with a reading buddy and read more of the story on their own. They spend a few minutes discussing the main idea and write down their reactions and responses to the events. In the photo below Ty and Alex share a book.

Dates for your calendar

January 23 - Tuesday
  Science field trip to Rocky hill
  wear shoes, class t-shirt, hat
  8:30-10:00 AM

February 1 - Thursday
  Science field trip to Makiki
  Stream, 12:45-2:00 PM
  wear shoes, class t-shirt

February 2 - Friday, Carnival
  Early release 11:20 AM

February 5 - no school
  Curriculum Day

February 19 - no school
  Presidents' Day

Progress Reports

Progress reports will be sent home with the students. They will not be mailed. So check your child's back pack. We hope to have all forms ready by next Friday, January 26th. If there is a delay, you will be notified.

You are asked to read over the report and fill in your perspective of your child's progress on the comment page. Then **return only the comment page to school by Friday, 2/2.** A copy will be made for your child's records, and the original sent home.

Figure 4–7. Class Newsletter.

© Punahou School, Honolulu, Hawai'i

Photo: Hannah and Wendiann take turns reading <u>Robinson Crusoe</u>. Then they take time to write their thoughts about the story.

Jump Rope for Heart

If your child has not earned their $1 for Jump Rope for Heart, please remind them that they need to do so by Friday, 1/26. That is when all monies and forms need to be returned to school.

The Art and Craft of Writing

The children continue to amaze me with how far they have come in writing. They are developing more ideas, and trying tools to enhance their pieces. We practice,
 • description, using all your senses,
 • slowing down the action. so we can see each detail of the movement,
 • dialogue, where characters bring scenes to life through their talking,
 • onomatopoeia, words that imitate sounds, buzz, crackle, clink
 • alliteration, words that begin with the same sound, "silent slithering snake,"
 • repetition, repeating certain words or phrases to emphasis ideas, "back and forth, back and forth across the floor."

These are some of the elements that help the children to stretch their writing skills. On the next page you can see some examples of "showing not telling." The students were asked to choose a sentence they had written and change it from telling to showing.

You can see by the examples, how much richer the writing became. Stephen King writes in his book <u>On Writing, a Memoir of the Craft</u> (2000), *"Description is what makes the reader a sensory participant in the story. Good description is a learned skill, one of the prime reasons why you cannot succeed unless you read a lot and write a lot."*
We are learning a lot, but it's hard work, and takes time and patience.

Robinson Crusoe (continued from p. 1)

We want the children to think as they read, question, critique, and make connections between the ideas in a piece of literature. When they are able to extend their thinking beyond the text, and share messages, connections to their experiences, or other books they have read, we know they have truly read, understood, and grown.

To help us reach this goal, we do several things:
 • choose good literature, ones that have strong characters, wonderful language, lessons or experiences that can lead us to see ourselves or our lives in new ways,
 • read aloud parts of the story, so they can hear the language, visualize the characters, and feel the excitement build,
 • share our thinking, not just what retelling what happened, but noting parts that confuse us, cause us to laugh, or raise questions - I wonder why that happened or that doesn't make sense.
 •allow enough time when reading so that we can read and share. When we rush through the reading, or have to stop too often, we lose the meaning, the feeling, the magic of the story.

We hope our literature studies open doors to reading that will last a lifetime.

Figure 4–7. (continued)

Figure 4–8. Student Sharing Progress Folio with Family.

Now that the children are ready and the parents have been nurtured to see learning and their child in a wider perspective, we bring them together for student-led conferences. Parents are given reminders that the focus of the conference is to listen, ask questions, and provide praise and encouragement for improved learning. Parents are also asked to send in any specific concerns that they want discussed beforehand, so the student and teacher can talk about these concerns prior to the conference and prepare responses (see Appendix C, Figure C-11).

Student-led conference logistics and time schedules vary from school to school. We usually have thirty minutes to meet with each parent. Twenty minutes is spent in a student-led format, and the remaining ten minutes are set aside for parent issues, usually questions such as "What else can I do to help my child?" If less time is available, conference planning forms can be modified and some of the sharing from the progress folio can be completed at home rather than at the conference. The challenge for us is to find time to share responsibility for assessment and evaluation with our students. Although it may be difficult, we try to use the following list as our guide:

- Replace busywork with more meaningful student-chosen activities.
- Replace testing with more self-evaluation and goalsetting.
- Replace lecturing with more shared discussion.

- Replace whole-class work with more small-group activities.
- Replace competition with collaboration and cooperation.

Implementing student-centered evaluation practices means looking at your curriculum, instruction, and assessment to see where students needs come first. This is a step many teachers hesitate to take because it removes control from their hands. It means they need to trust their students and set student needs before scope-and-sequence charts. It means being knowledgeable about curriculum and fitting it around student interests and inquiry. It means not being afraid to become a learner in your own classroom.

5

Bridging Assessment and Evaluation Across the Grades

- What Do We Mean by Standards?
- When Do Standards Hurt Kids?
- When Do Standards Help Kids?
- How Do We Match Assessment Tools with Standards?
- What Are Rubrics and How Do We Use Them?
- How Do We Fit in Report Cards?
- What About Standardized Tests?

What Do We Mean by Standards?

When we speak of standards in education, we are referring to the learning expectations we have for all students. What do we think all students should know, be able to do, and care about? When we answer this question, we are defining our standards.

Standards are meant to help students, teachers, and parents by providing clear expectations for learning. They act as a guide to measure student achievement and plan professional development opportunities for teachers to help develop more effective curricula and instructional strategies.

Standards place accountability upon students, educators, schools, and districts, and standards work toward educational equity for all. In essence, standards are aimed at making our schools better places for learning.

Unfortunately, many in positions of leadership have taken the call for standards as their crusade and have urged the passing of state standards so narrow that many students cannot meet them, and teachers will again bear the blame for their failures. We need to be aware, as Susan Ohanian says, of the "political agenda camouflaged as academic excellence" (1999, 12). To understand the issues behind standards, we need to know what standards are, what they can do to help children, what they can do that may hurt children, and what we can do about it.

When Do Standards Hurt Kids?

Susan Ohanian (1999), Alfie Kohn (1999, 2000), and others critical of the standards, urge us to be cautious about supporting standards if their only focus is to raise test scores. Kohn calls these *vertical standards*, where we just expect students to work harder and do more in order to "raise the bar." At the same time, schools afraid of failing to meet these higher expectations end up sacrificing meaningful learning experiences in order to have more time to prepare students for the test. Other criticisms of standards-based reform include:

- *Curriculum as a "bunch of facts."* Standards that overemphasize the learning of skills and facts in isolation means there is less time being focused on knowledge and understanding, less time spent thinking. (See Kohn 1999, 2000; Ohanian 1999; Routman 2000.)
- *Choices are dictated for teachers.* When standards specify methodology for teachers, they imply that teachers "need guardians and gatekeepers, and are incapable of making their own curriculum decisions . . . and attempt to strip teachers of their knowledge, their intuition, their pragmatic savviness, their flexibility, their very hearts" (Ohanian 1999, 101).
- *'All children will be able to' Statements.* When these statements are part of grade-by-grade standards, they ignore the individual differences among children and the different rates at which they develop.
- *Inequities in access to opportunities.* When all children are expected to meet or exceed standards, we disregard the fact that all kids are not equal. Nor do they have equal access to opportunities that enable school success. Children living in poverty and attending substandard schools, as well as those who speak English as a second language, do not receive the resources needed to give them a chance to succeed.
- *Standards are difficult to use.* Often standards use language that is vague and that does not make sense to teachers and parents. Content standards—what students should know—are listed, but performance standards—guidelines on how to assess if a child meets the standard—are not.

Being aware of the problems with standards may leave teachers feeling frustrated and defeated. But this is not the whole picture; there are ways we can define standards so that we can focus on and foster learning that benefits both teachers, parents, and students.

When Do Standards Help Kids?

The issue of standards is complex, and leads to confusion among teachers and parents. If we go back to the main aim of education, however, we see a broader goal for standards. They would produce people who are:

1. happy and fulfilled,
2. successful and productive,
3. ethical and decent,
4. independent and self-reliant, but also caring and compassionate, and
5. confident, curious, creative, critical thinkers, and good communicators. (Kohn 1999, 115)

The standards that would help kids reach these goals would be created by the people closest to them, who know them and their needs best—their teachers, parents, and communities. Student-centered standards would also take into account what we know about the diversity in our children, the multiple ways in which they learn, and include, rather than exclude, their rich cultural backgrounds and languages. Most of all, these standards would focus on improving learning and not punishing failure.

Teachers and the School Community Create Student-Centered Standards

Regie Routman (2000) reminds us that "we need to have conversations about what is worth knowing, understanding, and doing in our schools, districts, and communities if we are to work together to support the successful learning for all our students" (585). From these conversations we can begin to identify what matters in teaching and learning. In 1998, people from our school communities were brought together to work on the State of Hawai'i Content Standards. Each curriculum area had its own committee made up of university professors, elementary teachers, teachers from middle and secondary schools, parents, and representatives of Special Education and English as a Second Language. The diversity of each advisory board ensured that no one would be left out of the discussion.

Anna Sumida remembers working on a committee to draft the Content Standards for Language Arts. The first question they had to answer was, "What's important about the teaching and learning of reading?" Ideas that from that discussion included:

- Children love to read!
- Inquiry and ownership.
- Students problem solve and think creatively.

- Students engaged in learning.
- Students read widely and are exposed to many genres and books.
- Children learn all their basic conventions and skills.
- Students think open-mindedly about alternative stances on issues and opinions.
- Experiential teaching and hands-on approaches.
- Learning by doing; learning by teaching, and responsive teaching.
- Awareness of developmental stages of learning and reading.
- Students and teachers feel they have the authority to make changes.
- Open-ended responses to literature promote thinking.
- Multiple ways of thinking, expressing, and creating.
- A wide range of books can be made available to classrooms.
- Collaborative and social contexts for learning; dialogue is important to stimulate thinking.
- Ownership: self-selected books to read, goalsetting, and participation in evaluation.
- Reading is focused on meaning making.
- Teachers and students can use text to support ideas.
- Students who share books with others form a community of readers.

After the ideas were listed and discussed, they were sorted and grouped according to similar themes. Each set of ideas was labeled and then formed into six content strands. From each category, the standards were set to represent a shared understanding of what mattered in reading for the education communities in Hawai'i (see Figure 5–1). The entire State of Hawai'i Language Arts Content Standards can be found in Appendix A.

Student-Centered Standards Consider What Is Developmentally and Culturally Appropriate for Children

Standards, which are developmentally appropriate, should honor the way that children learn. This means that children need:

- rich contexts for learning that value their questions, wonderings, noticings, and inventions;
- multiple pathways and entry points that are appropriate to their different strengths and styles of learning, as well as their different cultural and linguistic backgrounds;
- teaching that builds on what they care about;
- time to make connections within their own thoughts;
- time to actively discover relatedness among events;

Reading and Literature

RANGE	Students will read a range of literary and informative texts for a variety of purposes.
PROCESSES	Students will use strategies within the reading processes to construct meaning.
CONVENTIONS AND SKILLS	Students will apply knowledge of the conventions of language and texts to construct meaning.
RESPONSE AND RHETORIC	Students will respond to texts from a range of stances: initial understanding, personal, interpretive, and critical.
ATTITUDES AND ENGAGEMENT	Students will demonstrate confidence as readers, and find value and satisfaction in reading and sharing reading experiences with others.
DIVERSITY	Students will interact thoughtfully and respectfully with texts that represent diversity in language, perspective, and/or culture.

Figure 5–1. Language Arts Content Standards.

- time for expressing, questioning, likening, remembering, appreciating, enjoying, discerning, and imagining, which leads to the development of deep understanding. (Falk 2000, 157)

Standards built upon a "bunch of facts" curriculum that measures what all students will be able to do grade by grade don't meet the criteria for being developmentally appropriate for many children. Toward this end, Alfie Kohn (1999) suggests that we need to think about *horizontal standards*, which serve as guidelines for shifting our teaching and learning. These broad guidelines of intellectual competence are more helpful to teachers and students than lists of facts and skills. Because the standards are broad, they leave specific curriculum and instructional decisions at the local level.

Appendix A shows an example from the Hawai'i Reading and Literature Grade Cluster Benchmarks for grades K–1, 2–3, and 4–5, which identify:

what students should know and be able to do at critical points of development during their elementary years. These benchmarks are specific enough to enable users of the standards to understand what students need to learn. While they do not mandate particular instructional approaches or instructional materials, they make clear what is expected of students. (Language Arts Content Standards 1999, 6)

As far as setting standards that are culturally appropriate, Hawai'i prides itself on being the "melting pot of the Pacific." Besides having citizens from many parts of the United States who reside on our islands, we are home to many cultural groups, such as Asians, Filipinos, Pacific Islanders, and Europeans. Our children are proud of their multiple nationalities—Chinese-Hawaiian and Portuguese-Spanish-Japanese, to name a few. We acknowledge these different cultures by honoring many traditions, stories, foods, clothing, holidays, and often languages in our classrooms. We recognize that understanding the perspectives of others is important for citizens of the future. To ensure that this value is not lost, we have identified a content strand for diversity in our Content Standards for Language Arts.

Student-Centered Standards Focus on Improving Student Learning

In order for standards to improve student learning, students need to know and understand what is expected of them. In our classrooms, we talk about standards with our students when we discuss good readers, writers, and mathematicians. We identify the knowledge, attitude, skills, and processes that lead to success. When we compared our own 'good readers' chart (see Figure 5–2) with the Hawai'i Language Arts Content Standards (1999), we noticed how well they aligned. These student statements can be considered *student-generated standards*, written in language they understand. While our chart lacks the specificity of the state standards, the goals remain the same.

Content Standards	Good Readers, Grade 2	Good Readers, Grade 5
Range *Students will read a range of literary and informative texts for a variety of purposes.	*Reads a variety of books.	*Chooses a variety books to read.
Processes *Students will use strategies within the reading process to construct meaning.	*Understands what they read; learns from their reading.	*Reads with understanding; makes connections.
Conventions and skills *Students will apply knowledge of the conventions of language and texts to construct meaning.	*Sounds out hard words; knows how to use punctuation.	*Reads fluently; sounds out words, uses other words in sentence, breaks words into parts.

Figure 5–2. Comparison of Student-Generated Standards with State of Hawai'i Content Standards.

When we bring teachers and school communities together to set standards that will make a difference in the lives of our children, we often end up trying to balance the tensions between external expectations and internal practices, between curriculum as a "bunch of facts" and curriculum that "leads to deep understandings about the world" (Falk 2000, 256), between schools where choices are dictated for teachers and schools that believe in the expertise of their teachers and provide them with resources for professional development and instructional improvement. "Standards, if done right, should not standardize what happens within schools. Rather, they should free the schools from top-down dictates while obliging them to focus on results" (Finn, Petrilli, and Vanourek 1998).

Gathering information that will help us see the results of student-centered standards requires that we select appropriate assessment tools for use throughout the school. Having common methods for assessing and evaluating student progress allows us to see growth over time, as students strive to meet expectations for academic success. Progress folios and student-involved conferences are two ways we share progress, but there are other practices, which are ongoing in our classrooms, that we use to find out how our students are doing and what we can do to help them.

How Do We Match Assessment Tools with Standards?

Before the State of Hawai'i defined its language arts standards, we were using our own set of teacher-generated standards for reading and writing. We drew upon our years of classroom experience, our knowledge of reading and writing, and our understanding of how children learn in order to create these statements. We didn't want to list of all of the skills and facts that students needed to be successful—we were interested in broad statements of competencies. We knew that if students were able to effectively meet the standards, we would see proficient use of appropriate skills and strategies in their performances. For instance, if a child were able to read fluently with expression, they were applying the necessary skills and knowledge of phonics, grammar, and meaning. If a student were writing effectively, we would expect to find qualities of good writing, such as organization of ideas, interesting leads, careful editing, and choice of words. So while there are numerous skills and knowledge that are needed for competent performance of the standards, these items are not standards in themselves.

When the State of Hawai'i Content Standards were published, we reviewed them to see how well our learning goals aligned with the state standards. We had already identified four main goals in our literacy program, as compared to the eighteen listed on the state document. However, we found that our teacher-generated standards could be found among the state standards (see Figure 5–3). This supports the notion that knowledgeable and experienced teachers know what

Teacher-Generated Standards	State of Hawaii Content Standards
* Students will read, comprehend, and respond critically, with deep understanding, to what they have read. This includes fiction and nonfiction material.	* Students will use strategies within the reading processes to construct meaning. (*Reading and Literature: Process Strand*) * Students will respond to texts from a range of stances: initial understanding, *personal, interpretive, and critical*. (*Reading & Literature: Response and Rhetoric Strand*)
* Students will demonstrate use of word identification skills in their oral reading by reading fluently with expression.	* Students will apply knowledge of the conventions of language and texts to construct meaning. (*Reading and Literature: Conventions and Skills*)
* Students will enjoy reading and share what they read with others. They will choose to read a variety of texts for a variety of purposes.	* Students will demonstrate confidence as readers, and find value and satisfaction in reading and sharing reading experiences with other. (*Reading and Literature: Attitudes and Engagement*) * Students will read a range of literary and informative texts for a variety of purposes. (*Reading and Literature: Range*)
* Students will be able to communicate thoughts, ideas, and feelings effectively when writing for a variety of purposes and audiences. They will use writing process and strategies appropriately.	* Students will write using various forms to communicate for a variety of purposes and audiences. (*Writing: Range*) * Students will use writing process and strategies appropriately and as needed to construct meaning and communicate effectively. (*Writing: Processes*) * Students will apply knowledge and understanding of the conventions of language and research when writing. (*Writing: Conventions and Skills*)

Figure 5–3. Comparison of Teacher-Generated Standards with State of Hawai'i Content Standards.

is best for their students, rather than legislators or people outside the schools who propose bills that mandate curriculum and methods.

Once we knew what we were working toward in terms of state standards, we needed to identify which assessment tools would provide us with the information we needed to monitor and improve student learning based on those learning goals. We also realized that if we wanted to look at our students' progress over a longer period of time, rather than at just the one year they were in our classes, we needed to have assessments that were consistent *across* the grade levels as well as *within* grade levels. For instance, it would not help if some teachers used end-of-chapter questions provided in basal curriculum guides and other teachers used more open-ended responses. These two examples would give different information on what students understood from their reading. To help us develop consistency among and within grades, we used common methods for gaining insight into our students' learning.

Returning to what experts (Bridges 1995; Davies 2000) tell us about assessing student learning, we looked for ways to watch children in action, reviewed collections of children's work, and talked with and listened to children as they reflected on their learning. We looked for methods that would provide this range of information and align with our standards. We wanted methods to fit within our curriculum and instructional practices so that we could gain evidence from actual classroom performance. We found little use for information provided by yearly standardized tests because it often tested a "bunch of facts" or isolated skill proficiency but had no value for understanding how children used their skills and knowledge to solve a problem or create a product of their learning. Figure 5–4 shows the assessment tools we found that would best meet our needs.

So we relied on our observation skills and took anecdotal notes of what children did in the process of reading and writing. Kathleen and James Strickland (2000, 21) recognize that teachers who assess by observation on a daily basis search for patterns in behavior, support children as they take risks and move forward, and watch to better facilitate further learning. They use conversations with the children and checklists and notes to record information, which helps them to draw conclusions about their children.

Another opportunity for assessment by observation occurred when we watched children reading aloud. With children in first grade, we use the Running Record procedures developed by Marie Clay (1993, 24). Teachers record "everything that a child says and does as he tries to read" from a book that has been chosen for them. Usually these texts are at the level the child is working on, but can be slightly harder so we can gain insights into how they process and problem solve when reading becomes difficult. With training and practice, teachers can become adept at noticing more about the reading behaviors of their students, and at using recording conventions, which help to analyze what they have observed and to plan appropriate interventions to assist that student's reading development. For more information on procedures and recording convention for Running Records see Clay's book *An Observation Survey of Early Literacy Achievement* (1993).

With students in second grade or higher, Reading Miscue Inventory procedures are used. In both Running Records and Reading Miscue Inventories, teachers listen

Teacher-Generated Standards	Watch Children in Action	Look at Collections of Children's Work	Talk with and Listen to Children Reflect on Their Learning
Students will read, comprehend, and respond critically to what they have read.	anecdotal notes of participation in literature discussions	written responses to literature: literature logs or journals	conferencing with children to discuss self-evaluation of literature study
Students will demonstrate use of word identification skills in their oral reading by reading fluently with expression.	Running Records (Clay) or Reading Miscue Inventory (Goodman, Watson, and Burke)	audiotapes of children reading	discuss results of Running Record or Reading Miscue Inventory with child
Students will enjoy reading and share what they read with others.	anecdotal notes of book sharing, time spent reading	reading logs	review reading logs to see what children notice about the reading choices they make
Students will be able to communicate thoughts, ideas, and feelings effectively when writing for a variety of purposes and audiences.	anecdotal notes of children's sharing of writing	writing pieces: final products as well as drafts	writing conferences, as well as self-evaluation of writing piece

Figure 5–4. Matching Assessment Tools with Standards.

to students read a selection out loud as they note miscues. A *miscue* is defined as an "observed response that does not match what the person listening to the reading expects of her" (Goodman, Watson, and Burke 1987, 37). By analyzing miscues, teachers are able to identify possible ineffective reading strategies being used by readers, and provide specific instruction to improve reading.

We kept collections of student work, such as written responses to literature, reading logs, and writing projects. Our language arts curriculum was built on a philosophy of student choice—grand conversations about literature (Peterson and Eeds 1990)—and responding with our interpretations (Rosenblatt 1993; Short

1997). More than just retelling what they remembered from their reading, students offered their opinions and understandings.

For example, at the end of their literature study of Mildred Taylor's books, JoAnn's second-grade class wrote their final comments on either *The Gold Cadillac* or *Song of the Trees*. In addition to writing a short summary of the book, the children were encouraged to think about what was important to them about the book. Following is Johnny's response after reading and discussing *Song of the Trees*:

> Mildred Taylor wrote a book called *Song of the Trees*. The main idea was that Mr. Anderson tells Big Ma he wants to cut down some of their trees for sixty-five dollars. But he's lying! He's going to cut down all the trees for a lousy sixty-five dollars. If Big Ma doesn't let him cut the trees Papa might have an accident.
>
> In the story there are four children. The oldest one is Stacey. Then came Cassie, she is the main character. Then came Christopher John, he was the one who ate too much. And Little Man was the one who liked to dress up. Big Ma, who owned the land, was their grandma. Papa is in Louisiana laying down tracks for the railroad.
>
> The problem is that Mr. Anderson wants to cut the trees down. Cassie thinks the trees can sing and she tries to tell Big Ma that Mr. Anderson is trying to rip them off. The solution is that Stacey goes and gets Papa. He comes with a black box that triggers dynamite and he says that if the white men don't leave and get out of their forest, he will blow up the forest. The men leave.
>
> I think that Papa did the right thing because white people were always treating the black people poorly. They didn't care about the black people because they thought they weren't normal. I think Papa stood up for his rights.

Writing workshop was another important part of our language arts period. Students kept notebooks where they recorded memories, images, ideas, or stories that they wanted to collect. From these collections, they later selected ideas that were important to them and began to develop those ideas into writing. Stories, research projects, and poetry collections were drafted, revised, discussed in conferences, and then edited before final sharing with the class. Every step of the process was kept and stored in students' folders so that we would have a complete record of writing development.

Talking with and listening to children as they reflected on the learning occurred naturally in our classrooms as the whole class met to review completed projects and also individually as student self-evaluations were discussed. Sometimes we would have a copy of a student's self-evaluation form included in their student folder as evidence of learning. Other times, a self-evaluation was just listed as an anecdotal note on a class list or an individual student record sheet.

Many times, we found that students would offer more thoughts and ideas in our conferences than they alluded to in their brief write-ups. Stephanie, a third grader, had chosen to do a project on pilgrims. She struggled in finding information, had difficulty writing up her ideas, and generally felt like she had done a bad job. On her self-evaluation sheet, she wrote down that this was a hard project and she wished she had more time. When she met with her teacher to go over the project evaluation, Stephanie revealed that it was her parents who wanted her to research the pilgrims. They took her to the library to get books, but the books they chose were much too hard for her to understand. She and her teacher agreed that on the next project Stephanie should choose something she was interested in, and they would find resources together. The teacher would also talk with Stephanie's parents about these changes. Stephanie's next project was on dolphins and she did a remarkable job!

We continue to keep students at the center of their learning, even when assessing their progress toward meeting standards, by selecting assessment tools that honor the many ways students can show what they know and what they can do. By agreeing to use the same assessment tools we also brought consistency and some continuity to progress folios across the grades.

We learned from our work with children, however, that without specific criteria to use in evaluating the evidence collected, students were not able to make sense of all the information and decide on the next steps for their learning. That led us to develop rubrics, or quality expectations, to use with our assessments. Accompanying these rubrics were examples of student work, so that together with students and parents we would know what constitutes excellence.

What Are Rubrics and How Do We Use Them?

It is not enough to tell our students to "do their best" and to "work harder." Work harder at what? Who decides what is our best? Talking with students about our expectations, detailing the essential features of an assignments or task, making a task as clear as possible so that they know what to do in order to succeed—this is the role rubrics play for us. Rubrics are a set of criteria for scoring or rating a student's test, portfolios, or performances. It is not "intended as checklist of completed items, but a guide to quality" (Bridges 1995, 42). Heidi Goodrich (1997) outlines some steps for designing rubrics with our students:

1. Look at models; show students examples of good and not-so-good work. Identify the characteristics of each example.
2. List criteria; use the discussion of the models to begin a list of what counts in quality work.
3. Articulate gradations of quality; describe the best and worst levels of quality, then fill in the middle levels.

4. Practice on models; have students use the rubrics to evaluate the models you gave them in the first exercise.
5. Use self- and peer assessment; give students their task, then as they work stop them occasionally for self- and peer assessment.
6. Revise; always give students time to revise their work based on the feedback they receive.
7. Use teacher assessment; use the same rubrics students used to assess their work yourself.

JoAnn followed a process similar to the one described by Goodrich to have her second-grade students develop a rubric for writing. She needed to provide the criteria, but the students showed what they knew about good writing as they came up with the descriptors in each box (see Figure 5–5).

As students become comfortable assessing their work with rubrics and making revisions based on feedback from their peers and teachers, we collect work samples. When we agree that a piece of student writing meets the expectation of a good piece of work, we look at the descriptors on the rubrics and comment on how the work matches up to the quality expectations. Figure 5–6 is a writing piece by Emily, a second grader. She was told this story by her grandmother on the day Pearl

	OK	Good	Excellent
Writing has good ideas.	• Not clear what you are trying to say. • Not enough ideas or information. • Some parts don't make sense.	• Has some good ideas. • Makes sense. • Some parts could be clearer.	• Good ideas that are explained well. • Gives readers a clear picture in their minds.
Writing is interesting.	• Not very interesting. • Little detail or description.	• Some parts are interesting and have good detail and description.	• Good detail and description. • Uses good words to show ideas. • Reader gets strong feeling or picture.
Writing looks good.	• Hard to read. • Many mistakes. • Needed more work editing.	• Most spelling is correct. • Most punctuation is correct. • Some paragraphs.	• Very few mistakes in spelling or punctuation. • Good use of paragraphs.

Figure 5–5. Rubrics for Good Writing.

December 7, 1941, Sunday around 8:00 AM my family and I climed on top of the third floor roof. We all said, "Wow, the practice at Pearl Harbor looks real." We saw ships going up in smoke. Airplanes wer buzzing around.

We went to Sunday School and the Reverend was standing in front of the church. He was listening to the radeo. The news sed this was war!

As we were rushing home we herd a loud BANG! The army's cannon went off in the wrong direction. All the action was at the military bases. It was a very frigtening day.

Writing has good ideas:
"I like the action, but I wanted to know more about what happened to the family next."

Writing is interesting:
"I like when she tells about the ships going up in smoke and the airplanes buzzing. I could see it in my mind." (good detail and description)

Writing looks good:
"She needed to check her spelling again. She still has mistakes."

Figure 5–6. Emily's Writing Piece.

Harbor was bombed by the Japanese and wanted to write about it. She and her peers rated it as a good piece of writing (see her peers' descriptions). Based on their comments, she later went on to add more to this piece.

While the students actively engaged in learning to understand the expectations for quality performance and task completion, their parents also needed to understand what was expected. Student Learning Goals booklets, summarizing curriculum, goals, and quality expectations, were created by teachers to share with parents. Often these booklets were shared and discussed at open house, so parents had time to review them before the first student-led conference. While the students were learning to explain their progress, goals, and challenges, aided by their version of rubrics, parents were shown how to use the Student Learning Goals booklet to see the next steps toward improving their child's learning. (An example from the Student Learning Goals booklet discussing reading can be found in Appendix B.)

Rubrics help make it possible for all students to complete good work because they are informed of exactly what they need to do to reach that level of excellence. Rubrics should be used to support and evaluate learning with the hopes of bringing everyone success. Rubrics also can help when grades on report cards are required. We will look at this issue next as we continue to find ways to keep students involved in assessing, evaluating, and reporting their own progress.

How Do We Fit in Report Cards?

Progress folios and student-involved conferencing bring us closer to achieving congruence between our beliefs about learning and evaluation and our assessment and evaluation processes. However, in many schools, the report card—a key component of evaluation—does not reflect what is valued in our classrooms. While growth and progress are the focus of our daily instruction and classroom activities, student "achievement" is often recorded on report cards as a single letter grade. This contradiction between measuring growth of performance and achievement on a graded scale creates a struggle between honoring what we value—a child's ongoing growth—and ranked achievement. In order to resolve this conflict, we look for ways to make report cards fit into a learner-centered process. In doing this, we need to think about

- What is a report card?
- What should a report card communicate?
- What should a report card look like?

What Is a Report Card?

Our conversations with each other helped us to define our own beliefs about report cards. We believe the primary purpose of a report card is to provide feedback on progress toward learning goals and to identify additional work needed toward achieving those goals. We believe a report card should:

- honor the developmental nature of learning
- communicate learning as an active and ongoing process
- focus on what the child can do
- inform parents and interested persons of a student's learning and growth over time, like the progress folio
- include the voices of the child and parents

If we want to honor these beliefs, then we need to reevaluate our report cards by looking at the kinds of information they communicate to parents.

What Should a Student-Centered Report Card Communicate?

Our beliefs about report cards indicate that communicating progress toward learning goals, and identifying next steps toward achieving those goals, are important. We also want our students and their parents involved in the reporting process, honoring their perspectives of the learning that is taking place. This is consistent with what we have done in the progress folio and student-involved conference processes.

The primary audience for report cards are students and their parents, so we asked ourselves, "What do our parents want to know about their child's progress?" and "What do students need to know about their work and progress?" By brainstorming, reading, and gathering information from teachers and parents, we concluded, that:

Parents Want to Know...

- if the child has made progress
- their current performance in the basic subjects—reading, writing, mathematics
- areas where additional work is needed
- if grade level expectations are being met
- if the child is applying him- or herself
- if the child is "behaving" well

Children Want to Know That Their...

- hard work and efforts are recognized
- strengths are acknowledged
- weaknesses are seen as challenges, not deficits
- thoughts and opinions are valued

Our task is to come up with a report card that communicates our beliefs, provides relevant information to parents and other interested parties, is meaningful to our students, and allows for perspectives of students and parents to be represented. The report card should support continued improvement with specific feedback and descriptors of expectations. Traditional report cards with letter grades did not meet these needs for us, so redesigning our elementary report card was important if we truly wanted to focus our teaching, assessment, evaluation, and reporting on our student-centered practices.

What Would a Student-Centered Report Card Look Like?

Reviewing examples of nontraditional report cards, we notice rubrics, checklists of expected skills and strategies, and developmental continuums being used to report student performance. Terms such as *emerging, developing, practicing, independent,* and *proficient* are used to describe a student's level of achievement. The tone of these report cards recognizes developmental growth toward specific objectives, standards, and skills.

An example of the second-grade report card currently used at Punahou School is shown in Figure 5–7. For each curriculum area there are specific criteria identified. The ratings are based on a student working toward expectations, meeting

PUNAHOU SCHOOL

Student: Grade Two   Teacher: 2001-2002

K E Y		
1 = Not yet apparent:	The student has not yet been observed using this behavior.
2 = Working toward expectations :	The student attempts and shows interest in this behavior and experiments with correct usage.
3 = Meets expectations: (Uses effectively and efficiently)	"Effective" means using the behavior correctly to get things done. "Efficient" means that the behavior is performed without undue effort.
4 = Exceeds expectations:	The student takes initiative to apply and extend this behavior.

LANGUAGE ARTS	FALL				SPRING			
READING	1	2	3	4	1	2	3	4
1. Demonstrates understanding of text								
2. Extends understanding beyond text								
3. Uses a variety of word identification strategies to decode								
4. Reads frequently and independently for pleasure and to find information								
WRITING	1	2	3	4	1	2	3	4
5. Expresses ideas in writing								
6. Enhances writing with detail and vocabulary								
7. Uses writing as a tool for thinking and learning (journals, note taking, reflections)								
8. Uses mechanics of writing (punctuation, grammar, sentence structure, word usage)								
9. Makes effective use of spelling strategies								
HANDWRITING	1	2	3	4	1	2	3	4
10. Forms letters correctly								
11. Writes legibly								
ORAL LANGUAGE AND LISTENING SKILLS	1	2	3	4	1	2	3	4
12. Speaks clearly and audibly								
13. Uses adequate vocabulary to express ideas								
14. Listens attentively								
15. Follows directions								

Figure 5–7. Progress Report Form.

PUNAHOU SCHOOL

Student: **Grade Two**   **Teacher: Mr. Lum**   **2001-2002**

K E Y

1 = Not yet apparent:	The student has not yet been observed using this behavior.
2 = Working toward expectations:	The student attempts and shows interest in this behavior and experiments with correct usage.
3 = Meets expectations: (Uses effectively and efficiently)	"Effective" means using the behavior correctly to get things done. "Efficient" means that the behavior is performed without undue effort.
4 = Exceeds expectations:	The student takes initiative to apply and extend this behavior.

MATHEMATICS

	FALL				SPRING			
	1	2	3	4	1	2	3	4
16. Demonstrates understanding of concepts								
17. Applies concepts								
18. Understands numbers and operations								
19. Uses a variety of problem solving strategies								
20. Expresses understanding of strategies (Orally, in writing, drawing, or with manipulatives)								

SCIENCE/SOCIAL STUDIES

	1	2	3	4	1	2	3	4
21. Understands concepts								
22. Integrates and relates ideas and information								

PERSONAL DEVELOPMENT

	1	2	3	4	1	2	3	4
Is a self-directed learner								
23. Is responsible and prepared								
24. Is resourceful in solving problems								
25. Uses unstructured time wisely								
26. Has a positive attitude								
27. Is self-directed and self-motivated								
28. Shows self confidence								
29. Participates in activities and discussions								
Is a collaborative worker								
30. Respects people, property, materials, and environments								
31. Behaves appropriately								
32. Cooperates and works well with others								
Is a quality producer								
33. Completes tasks in allotted time								
34. Keeps belongings and materials organized								
35. Accepts suggestions for improvement								

Figure 5–7. (continued)

PUNAHOU SCHOOL	
Student: Grade Two Teacher:	2001-02
Student Perspective	**Parent Perspective**
	Compliments:
	Wishes:
	Comments:
Signature:	Signature(s):

Figure 5–7. (continued)

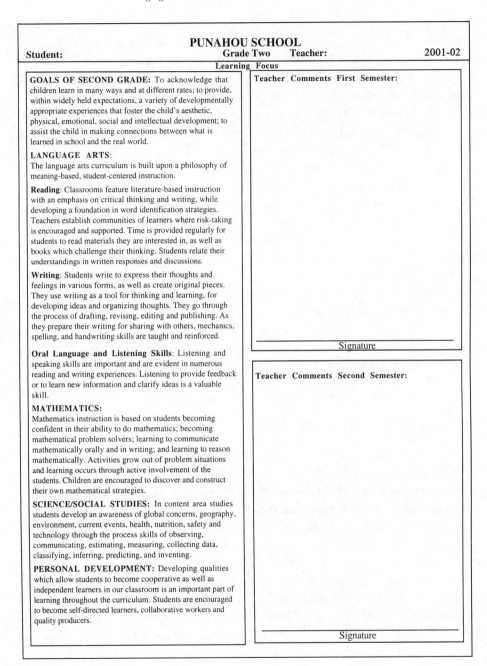

PUNAHOU SCHOOL

Student: **Grade Two**   **Teacher:**   2001-02

Learning Focus

GOALS OF SECOND GRADE: To acknowledge that children learn in many ways and at different rates; to provide, within widely held expectations, a variety of developmentally appropriate experiences that foster the child's aesthetic, physical, emotional, social and intellectual development; to assist the child in making connections between what is learned in school and the real world.

LANGUAGE ARTS:
The language arts curriculum is built upon a philosophy of meaning-based, student-centered instruction.

Reading: Classrooms feature literature-based instruction with an emphasis on critical thinking and writing, while developing a foundation in word identification strategies. Teachers establish communities of learners where risk-taking is encouraged and supported. Time is provided regularly for students to read materials they are interested in, as well as books which challenge their thinking. Students relate their understandings in written responses and discussions.

Writing: Students write to express their thoughts and feelings in various forms, as well as create original pieces. They use writing as a tool for thinking and learning, for developing ideas and organizing thoughts. They go through the process of drafting, revising, editing and publishing. As they prepare their writing for sharing with others, mechanics, spelling, and handwriting skills are taught and reinforced.

Oral Language and Listening Skills: Listening and speaking skills are important and are evident in numerous reading and writing experiences. Listening to provide feedback or to learn new information and clarify ideas is a valuable skill.

MATHEMATICS:
Mathematics instruction is based on students becoming confident in their ability to do mathematics; becoming mathematical problem solvers; learning to communicate mathematically orally and in writing; and learning to reason mathematically. Activities grow out of problem situations and learning occurs through active involvement of the students. Children are encouraged to discover and construct their own mathematical strategies.

SCIENCE/SOCIAL STUDIES: In content area studies students develop an awareness of global concerns, geography, environment, current events, health, nutrition, safety and technology through the process skills of observing, communicating, estimating, measuring, collecting data, classifying, inferring, predicting, and inventing.

PERSONAL DEVELOPMENT: Developing qualities which allow students to become cooperative as well as independent learners in our classroom is an important part of learning throughout the curriculum. Students are encouraged to become self-directed learners, collaborative workers and quality producers.

Teacher Comments First Semester:

_____
Signature

Teacher Comments Second Semester:

_____
Signature

Figure 5–7. (continued)

expectations, and exceeding expectations. To help parents understand the criteria and levels of achievement, rubrics for each area included on the report card are explained in the Student Learning Goals booklet (see Appendix B). The teacher also introduces students to these rubrics using language they can understand and examples to make them clear.

We realize many schools have little choice in the report cards they use. However, rubrics can be used with all report cards to clarify expectations, and also be used as the criteria for assigning grades when grades are called for.

Another important feature in moving toward student-centered report cards is including space for students to add their comments. Traditionally, it has been the teacher who writes the narratives that sum up important aspects of student achievement. With the shift toward more student and parent involvement, we realize that each party has something to contribute—students write about their strengths, challenges, and goals; parents share what they notice about their child's growth and their concerns. The second-grade progress report from Punahou School also includes these perspectives with a section for teacher comments, and an additional page for student and parent perpectives.

With the addition of rubrics and shared comment pages, we have made a strong statement about what we value in learning, and bring consistency and continuity to our teaching, assessment, evaluation, and reporting.

What About Standardized Tests?

In Hawai'i, like many other states, the standardized test scores of public schools are published in local newspapers. This, of course, leads to unfair comparisons between different districts and schools. Parents with young children scramble to get them into those institutions that perform well, often applying at schools outside their neighborhoods. They claim that the special programs their child needs are not available at their schools, and use geographic exceptions to place their child elsewhere. Often, on the basis of this one measure, schools gain or lose support in the community.

Schools need to be held accountable, so politicians often suggest that standardized test results offer that proof. While this statement has not been linked directly to school funding, teachers still feel the pressure to raise scores. Many teachers are stressed because they are not receiving the help they need to meet school or state expectations. In Hawai'i, we have made some good first steps with the writing of our content standards, but the implementation of the standards in classrooms has been slowed due to the lack of support and proper training needed to connect standards to instruction.

Like other schools across our nation, teachers spend additional time in test preparation—how to read the questions, what strategies to use for multiple choice tests, or worse, teaching to the test. Money is spent purchasing practice tests, and valuable learning time is used for working through the practice booklets and correcting errors. Even more open-ended tests, like the Stanford 9, require teachers to spend time teaching their students strategies for making clear responses with explanations that show their critical thinking skills. Another problem with open-ended tests is scoring them—because special training is required, these tests often need to be sent to special scoring centers so the results will be reliable. This incurs additional expenses for the schools.

Why so much emphasis on standardized tests? Alfie Kohn (2000) suggests that there are several parties who are very interested in standardized measures. Those who:

- want traditional "back to basics" instruction
- are against public schools and for privatization of education
- want to make a profit from the manufacturing and scoring of tests (including publishers who create and promote materials that "guarantee to raise test scores")
- want to get ahead politically by "raising the bar" with their call for higher standards.

If standardized tests are time-consuming for teacher and students and an added expense for our schools, do the results benefit students and teachers? The answer is *no*. The information that guides a teacher's instruction comes from his or her continuous observations of children involved in meaningful activities. By "responding to what the child is trying to do" (Smith 1984, 24) we are able to meet their specific and unique needs.

The information that makes it possible for our children to move forward in their learning comes from regular, ongoing talks between teacher and student. These talks are often centered on work in progress, as children encounter challenges in learning. These discussions also include celebrations of work well done, and acknowledgments of what was hard and how difficulties were overcome. The next powerful talks are the ones that help students set new goals and strive for higher levels of success.

The information that helps parents understand the progress their children make does not come from standardized tests, but from looking at portfolios of work samples, from listening to their child talk about his or her learning at conferences, and from open communication with the teacher.

We have effective ways for improving student performance and communicating progress with parents that do not rely on standardized tests. But there are those legislators and administrators who want to use these measures to assess schools and districts. Alfie Kohn (2000, 47) offers this advice to them:

- Results of the tests should be looked at with reference to a given standard of achievement, not how one student is doing compared to other students (norm-referenced).
- Results should be evaluated in light of special challenges faced by a school or district. Large numbers of students with special needs, equal access to resources and materials, and minority and poverty situations need to be considered when evaluating test results.
- If we are assessing whole schools or districts, there is no reason to test every student. Instead, test a sampling of students representing a cross section of the school population.
- In addition to testing, we should also judge schools by visiting them and looking for evidence of learning and interest in learning.

We need to educate ourselves, as well as our parents and administrators, about standardized tests. By understanding what information they do provide and what they don't, we can argue for more effective methods of student assessment and evaluation. With this knowledge, we can create systems for accountability that lead to successful school reform. We want to make schools better places for our children, and this will require the rethinking of standardized testing itself (Kohn 2000, 66).

Final Reflections

As we reflect on what led us to the changes in our teaching, several key points come to mind. We hope they will be helpful to teachers beginning this journey:

- We were uncomfortable with the way our assessment and evaluation practices did not support the learning going on in the classroom.
- We wanted to see more continuity and consistency.
- We felt we needed to change things.

Are there things that raise questions for you in your classroom? Do they make you a little uneasy, angry, or frustrated? This may be the starting point for you.

- We had questions and began to seek out answers.
- We read professional literature, attended workshops, and took university courses to help us build our knowledge of ideas, strategies, and procedures to make the necessary changes.

Are there professional development opportunities available in your education community? Start to read professional literature in your area of interest. In *Conversations* (2000), Regie Routman provides excellent resources for teachers in her Blue Pages.

- Making change is hard, but it can be made easier when there are others who are interested in pursuing the same cause. Our group started with teachers who wanted to talk about writing. From these initial discussions, we shared our beliefs about learning, which led to this project.

Are there others in your school who have expressed the same frustrations or concerns as you? Find a support group or a supportive person, either in your school or in your education community, to talk with. This will help clarify your questions and refine your ideas.

- Perhaps the hardest issue of all is time—having the time to experiment and to reflect and revise our practices on top of our regular teaching load. We constantly modified our lessons, discussions, prompts, forms, and procedures as we found what worked best with our students. There were many times when things did not go well, so we took a step back and reflected on what happened. Then we tried again.

Things will not work perfectly all the time. But take the time to make those first steps and see how it works with your children. *Adapt, not adopt* our procedures if they don't work. Give yourself time to learn just as you give that time to your students.

From our partnership with children and their parents, we have witnessed renewed enthusiasm for learning in our students. As teachers, we have found new energy for our work with children. It has not been easy, nor do we do things exactly the same way every year. We learn through conversations with our colleagues, by reading professional literature that presents us with new ideas to try, and by paying close attention to our students. We watch, listen, assess, document, analyze, reflect, and respond in ways that address the needs of each child. This is the most effective way to teach and evaluate. We adjust and adapt our procedures, but the heart of our work remains the same: Children and their needs, interests, questions, hopes and dreams always come first.

Appendix A

Strands	Reading & Literature	Writing	Oral Communication
RANGE	1. Students will read a range of literary and informative texts for a variety of purposes.	1. Students will write using various forms to communicate for a variety of purposes and audience.	1. Students will communicate orally using various forms—interpersonal, group, and public—for a variety of purposes and situations.
PROCESSES	2. Students will use strategies within the reading processes to construct meaning.	2. Students will use writing processes and strategies appropriately and as needed to construct meaning and communicate effectively.	2. Students will use strategies within speaking and listening processes to construct and communicate meaning.
CONVENTIONS AND SKILLS	3. Students will apply knowledge of the conventions of language and texts to construct meaning.	3. Students will apply knowledge and understanding of the conventions of language and research when writing.	3. Students will apply knowledge of verbal and nonverbal language to communicate effectively.
RESPONSE AND RHETORIC	4. Students will respond to texts from a range of stances: initial understanding, personal, interpretive, and critical.	4. Students will use rhetorical devices to craft writing appropriate to audience and purpose.	4. Students will adapt messages appropriate to audience, purpose, and situation.
ATTITUDES AND ENGAGEMENT	5. Students will demonstrate confidence as readers, and find value and satisfaction in reading and sharing reading experiences with others.	5. Students will demonstrate confidence as writers, and find value and satisfaction in writing and sharing writing with others.	5. Students will demonstrate confidence as communicators, and find value and satisfaction in communicating with others.
DIVERSITY	6. Students will interact thoughtfully and respectfully with texts that represent diversity in language, perspective, and/or culture.	6. Students will understand diversity in language, perspective, and/or culture in order to craft texts that represent diverse thinking and expression.	6. Students will understand diversity in language, perspective, and/or culture and use speaking and listening to foster understanding.

The eighteen Language Arts Content Standards are organized into six strands across three components of the language arts. The standards represent a necessary mix of cognitive, intellectual, academic, and practical dimensions of learning. While the standards emphasize the academic performance and intellectual accomplishments of Hawai'i's students, they also acknowledge that learning has a social and emotional component.

Figure A–1. State of Hawai'i Language Arts Content Standards.

Content Standards	K–1	2–3	4–5
RANGE 1. Read a range of literary texts for a variety of purposes.	• Read narrative and informative texts. • Read for enjoyment and to gain information. • Read and follow simple directions to perform tasks.	• Read both fiction and nonfiction. • Read for enjoyment and to gain information. • Read and apply information and directions to perform tasks.	• Read a variety of genres. • Read for literary experience and to develop aesthetic appreciation. • Read to research a topic. • Read information and instructions to perform tasks and solve problems.
COMPREHENSION PROCESSES 2. Use strategies within the reading processes to construct meaning.	• Make reasonable predictions about what will happen in a story. • Draw on personal experiences and prior knowledge to comprehend text. • Select and organize information to tell a story.	• Make conscious connections between prior knowledge and text while reading to construct meaning. • Verify and clarify ideas by referring to text. • Recognize breakdowns in comprehension and repair these breakdowns by rereading, asking questions, and seeking clarification. • Relate critical facts and details in narrative or informational text to comprehend text.	• Infer ideas from text. • Modify initial interpretation in light of new information and prior experience. • Recognize breakdowns in comprehension, and repair these breakdowns by asking questions, seeking clarification, and summarizing. • Integrate important information gathered from a long passage or text to interpret meaning.
CONVENTIONS AND SKILLS 3. Apply knowledge of the conventions of language and texts to construct meaning.	• Show knowledge of the foundations of literacy—concepts of print, phonemic awareness, experience with text—when reading. • Apply letter knowledge and spelling-sound word recognition strategies to decode unknown words in text. • Demonstrate increasing fluency, including the ability to read frequently occurring words by sight.	• Demonstrate fluent reading of grade-appropriate texts, applying spelling–sound word recognition strategies and meaning-based word recognition strategies as appropriate. • Apply knowledge of suffixes, prefixes, and word parts as meaningful cues to words. • Apply knowledge of fiction and nonfiction genres to understand text.	• Use knowledge of story elements (e.g., character, setting, mood, incident, structure) to interpret text. • Differentiate between literal and figurative language and infer appropriate meaning when reading.

Figure A–2. Hawai'i Language Arts Content Standards (1999) Reading and Literature Grade Cluster Benchmarks.

Content Standards	K–1	2–3	4–5
RESPONSE 4. Respond to tests from a range of stances: initial understanding, personal, interpretive, critical.	• Identify favorite part of story and give reasons for choice. • Share information from text. • Interpret text through dramatization, writing, or art.	• Relate information and events in text to own ideas and life experiences. • State the important ideas from reading and identify a theme or generalization. • Interpret texts in a variety of ways (e.g., writing, drama, art, media).	• State the important ideas and interpret author's message, theme, or generalization. • Compare own ideas with ideas in text, and analyze similarities and differences. • Demonstrate a critical response by representing text in another form, genre, or medium.
ATTITUDES AND ENGAGEMENT 5. Demonstrate confidence as readers, and find value and satisfaction in reading and sharing reading experiences with others.	• Read on one's own for enjoyment. • Identify favorite books. • Share reading experiences with others.	• Identify favorite genres and topics for reading. • Read voluntarily for own purposes. • Share reading with others.	• Indicate preferences of reading materials and authors. • Read more about a topic on one's own and for own purposes.
DIVERSITY 6. Interact thoughtfully with texts that represent diversity in language, perspective, and/or culture.	• Read about others from different cultures to gain perspectives different from own.	• Share in the experiences of others from different cultures through reading and discussion.	• Interact thoughtfully with each other about texts that represent diverse perspectives.

Figure A–2. (continued)

Appendix B

Introduction

As I considered what I wanted to share with parents at open house, I reflected on what I value about teaching and learning. I think it is important for parents to know that I believe:

- All students can learn when they feel confident and supported by those around them.
- Students learn in many different ways, reflecting their individual styles, intelligences, and talents.
- Students need opportunities for learning where they are given responsibility for making choices, encouraged to collaborate with other learners, and have sufficient time to care and think deeply about what they are learning.
- The goal of education is independence, where students take responsibility for and are active participants in their own learning.
- Teachers should focus on children's strengths first, and show respect for the developmental level of each child.
- Teachers are facilitators, learners, mentors, leaders, and scholars, as well as role models for kindness.
- Evaluation is an ongoing part of learning, and it is important for students and teachers to share in this responsibility.

This booklet serves to share the goals for learning in our classroom and the expectations of performance in the language arts and mathematics curriculum. It also describes the qualities that help students become successful learners in life.

By sharing these expectations and goals with our students and parents, we form a partnership that supports academic achievement while also developing cooperative and collaborative skills essential for living and working in the world today.

—JoAnn Wong-Kam
Second-Grade teacher
Punahou School

Figure B–1. Student Goals Booklet, Pages 1–4.

Language Arts

In our language arts curriculum, our goal is to produce students who are confident, creative, critical thinkers, and good communicators. In our reading and writing workshops, students are actively involved in reading and creating meaningful literature. With whole-class discussions, small-group work, and individual conferences as needed, the instruction is focused on meeting student needs while also challenging thinking to higher levels.

In reading workshop, students participate in literature circles[1] where they meet in small groups to read, write responses, and discuss the ideas and issues of literature as it relates to their lives and the world around them. We nurture their interest in reading by providing DEAR (Drop Everything and Read) time each day for them to read materials of their own choosing. Reading aloud to children is another regular part of our day. We would like students to become familiar with a wide range of books and authors.

Writing workshops start early in the year with an emphasis on students finding personal value in writing by sharing stories that are important to them. The teacher helps students identify significant topics to write about and encourage them to express their thoughts with the same richness and voice they find in the literature they read. The teacher develops the craft of writing through the use of the process approach to writing.[2,3] We present opportunities for a variety of writing—personal narratives, memoirs, poetry, and fiction, as well as research projects. As they prepare their writing for sharing, mechanics and spelling skills are taught and reinforced.

Listening and speaking skills are a valuable part of the numerous reading and writing experiences. Project presentations provide opportunities for formal speech performances, while small-group discussions invite the informal exchange of ideas. Listening to provide feedback and to learn new information is an important part of our work in school.

1. Short, Kathy, Jerome C. Harste, and Carolyn Burke. 1996. *Creating Classrooms for Authors and Inquirers*. Portsmouth, NH: Heinemann.
2. Graves, Donald. 1983. *Writing: Teachers and Children at Work*. Portsmouth, NH: Heinemann.
3. Graves, Donald. 1994. *A Fresh Look at Writing*. Portsmouth, NH: Heinemann.

Figure B–1. (continued)

Reading Goal

Students will be able to read, comprehend, and respond critically, with deep understanding, to what they have read. This includes fiction and nonfiction literature. Students will:

- demonstrate understanding of text
- extend understanding beyond text

Evidence for Evaluation

Evidence may include written responses to literature, anecdotal records, checklists/notes of literature discussions, and literature projects, which in turn may include art or other media.

Quality Expectations

	Working toward expectations	Meeting expectations (using effectively and efficiently)	Exceeding expectations
Comprehension Literal and inferential comprehension; demonstrate the relationship between their understanding and the text	• Recognize topic and can retell most of the main ideas or events.	• Can summarize text. • Can explain important ideas and include some details. • May not be able to explain relationships between ideas, characters or events.	• Demonstrate understanding of text by retelling, summarizing, or making notes. • Can refer to text to support inferences or interpretations. • Can draw connections between several different texts.
Response Connections between the text and an understanding of themselves and their world; synthesize ideas and evaluate what they read	• Make a personal response that is loosely connected to the text. • Can tell what they liked or disliked.	• Can reflect on what they have read and explain their ideas or feelings.	• Make connections to past knowledge and experiences. • Can evaluate text and offer reasons and explanations.

Revised 7/28/00

Source: *Evaluating Reading across Curriculum.* 1995. Province of British Columbia, Canada: Ministry of Education.

Figure B–1. (continued)

Student Statements: How Am I Doing as a Reader?

	Okay	Good	Excellent
Comprehension Do I understand what I read?	I know what this book is about.	My reading makes sense to me. Sometimes I have to go slowly or read parts over again. Although some parts may be confusing, I can tell you about the main ideas or events. If someone asks me a question, I can usually find the answer.	I can recall important facts and ideas, and find answers to questions. If I read a story I can tell about the characters and retell the main events and many of the details. When I read information or do research I can remember and share the main ideas and a lot of the details.
Response What do I think about what I have read?	This makes me think about something that happened to me—or maybe something I heard or watched. I can tell you if I liked what I read.	I can tell you what I read about, and remember some of the details and information. I can tell you what it reminds me of and how it's like other things I've read, heard, or seen.	I can talk or write about how what I read fits with my own ideas and experiences and other things I've read, seen, or heard. I can tell you how I feel about what I read and give you reasons for my feelings.

Example of a Good Response to Reading

Mildred D. Taylor wrote a book called *Song of the Trees*. The main idea was that Mr. Anderson tells Big Ma that he wants to cut down some of their trees for 65 dollars but he's lying. He's going to cut down all trees for a lousy 65 dollars. But if Big Ma doesn't let him cut down the trees Papa might have an accident.

In the story there are 4 children. The oldest one is Stacey. Then came Cassie, she is the main character. Then came Christopher John, he was the one who ate too much. And Little Man, who liked to dress up. Big Ma who owned the land and was their Grandma. Mr. Anderson, who wanted to cut down the trees for 65 dollars. Papa, who is in Louisiana laying tracks for the railroad.

The problem is Mr. Anderson wants to cut the trees down. Cassie thinks the trees can sing and she tries to tell Big Ma that they're ripping themselves off. The solution is that Stacey goes and gets Papa and he comes with a black box that triggers dynamite and he says that if the white men don't leave the logs here and get out of their forest, he will blow up the forest. The men leave without their logs.

Figure B–1. (continued)

I think that Papa did the right thing because white people were always treating black people very poorly. They don't care about black people because they thought that black people weren't normal like white people because they weren't rich and they didn't like them. I think Papa stood up for his rights.

Commentary

Comprehension

Student retells important ideas with some details but shows little understanding of relationship between ideas, characters, or events. For example, a student tells about a problem with Mr. Anderson, who wants to cut down trees without paying a fair price. She names the characters and tells how Papa comes home and threatens to blow up trees, but shows no understanding of characters relating to events and their actions.

Response

Student reflects on what she has read and explains her ideas or feelings. For example, some of this thinking is revealed when student tells how she feels Papa did the right thing by making some general statements about the conflict between black and white people. No references are made to the text to support her opinion.

Figure B–1. (continued)

Appendix C

Blackline Masters

Name:		Date:	
Goal:		Goal:	
Plan:		Plan:	

Name:		Date:	
Goal:		Goal:	
Plan:		Plan:	

Figure C–1. Goal and Action Plan Form.

© 2001 from *Elevating Expectations*. Portsmouth, NH: Heinemann.

Introducing . . .

Photo of child

I enjoy —————————————————

————————————————————————

————————————————————————

My favorite books are —————————————

————————————————————————

My favorite authors are ——————————

————————————————————————

My favorite games are —————————————

My favorite places to visit are ——————

————————————————————————

Ths is what I can do well: ————————

————————————————————————

In second grade I want ——————————

————————————————————————

Figure C–2. All About Me Page.

© 2001 from *Elevating Expectations*. Portsmouth, NH: Heinemann.

Name _____

Literature Sharing: Your child has just finished reading the book

_____

Tonight they will share the book with you and read you their favorite part.
Talk with them about the story. Then complete the sections below. Thank
you for participating in our literature sharing.

What I learned from the story

_____

_____

_____

_____

_____

_____

_____

What I thought of my child as a reader

_____

_____

_____

_____

_____

_____

_____

Figure C–3. Literature Sharing.

© 2001 from *Elevating Expectations*. Portsmouth, NH: Heinemann.

> Date: _____
>
> This is an example of. . .
>
> _____
>
> I want you to notice that. . .
>
> _____
>
> _____
>
> _____
>
> _____

Figure C–4. Self-Evaluation Form.

© 2001 from *Elevating Expectations*. Portsmouth, NH: Heinemann.

> As a writer,
>
> I think writing is —————————————— because
>
> _____
>
> _____
>
> As a writer I can do these things well,
>
> _____
>
> _____
>
> I can improve as a writer by,
>
> _____
>
> _____

Figure C–5. Writing Self-Evaluation Form.

© 2001 from *Elevating Expectations*. Portsmouth, NH: Heinemann.

Weekly Progress

Name: _____

Date: _____

My goal for the week is _____

_____

Monday _____ Assignments & Events	Feelings	Daily Reflection
_____		_____
_____		_____
_____		_____
_____		_____
_____		_____
_____		_____
Tuesday _____ Assignments & Events		Daily Reflection
_____		_____
_____		_____
_____		_____
_____		_____
_____		_____
Wednesday _____ Assignments & Events		Daily Reflection
_____		_____
_____		_____
_____		_____
_____		_____
_____		_____

Figure C–6. Weekly Progress Chart.

© 1994 from *Multi-Age and More*. Winnipeg, MB: Peguis Publishers Ltd.

Thursday_____ Assignments & Events	Feelings	Daily Reflection
_____		_____
_____		_____
_____		_____
_____		_____
_____		_____
_____		_____

Friday_____ Assignments & Events		Daily Reflection
_____		_____
_____		_____
_____		_____
_____		_____
_____		_____
_____		_____

How did I do this week?

student   _____

_____

teacher   _____

_____

parent comment

_____

_____

_____

Figure C–6. (continued)

© 1994 from *Multi-Age and More*. Winnipeg, MB: Peguis Publishers Ltd.

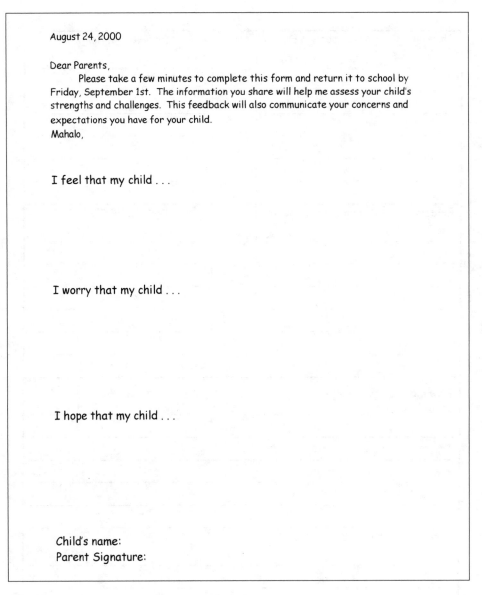

August 24, 2000

Dear Parents,
      Please take a few minutes to complete this form and return it to school by
Friday, September 1st. The information you share will help me assess your child's
strengths and challenges. This feedback will also communicate your concerns and
expectations you have for your child.
Mahalo,

I feel that my child . . .

I worry that my child . . .

I hope that my child . . .

Child's name:
Parent Signature:

Figure C–7. Parent Letter.

© 2001 from *Elevating Expectations*. Portsmouth, NH: Heinemann.

Name	Date

Progress Check: self-evaluation

One thing I have been trying to do well	Two things I am proud of
I need some help with	I want you to notice

Figure C–8. Progress Check.

© 2001 from *Elevating Expectations*. Portsmouth, NH: Heinemann.

Now that you have had a chance to explore your child's Progress Folio with him/her, please take a moment to talk to your child about the work you have seen. Ask questions about it, and give feedback to your child. Please start with the positives (two stars) and then move on to one "wish" (something you would like your child to work on next). Please be selective and realistic in your "wish."

A star _____

_____

A star _____

_____

A wish _____

_____

Parent's signature _____

Figure C–9. Progress Folio Comment Sheet.

© 2001 from *Elevating Expectations*. Portsmouth, NH: Heinemann.

Dear Parents,

Your child is bringing home work recently done in class. Your child has written a self-evaluation about this work, sharing what he or she has been trying to do well, two things he or she is proud of, and identifying something he or she would like help with.

Please take a few quiet minutes to listen and learn as your child shares his or her work samples with you. Celebrate areas of achievement and offer encouragement on the things your child finds challenging.

We are asking that you add your comments about your child's learning on the form below, and return the form and the work samples to school by _____.

Thank you for working with us to bring success to your child's learning.

Dear _____,

After looking at your work, we would like to compliment you on

We would like to support you as you continue to work on

_____

Comments or questions for the teacher

Figure C–10. Parent Comment Sheet.

© 2001 from *Elevating Expectations*. Portsmouth, NH: Heinemann.

Dear Parents,

We are looking forward to our student-teacher-parent conferences coming up. Your conference is scheduled for _____.

Here is what you can expect during the conference:

- You and your child will have some time to look at his/her assignments and displays around the classroom.

- Next your child will share his/her progress folio with us and explain his/her strengths and challenges and set new learning goals for the upcoming quarter.

- Your child is prepared to take an active part in our conference. There will be opportunities for you to ask questions, make comments, or express concerns.

- After the conference, I will write a summary of what was shared and send it home to you.

To help us prepare for the conference, please note any areas you would like to discuss below:

_____
_____
_____
_____
_____
_____
_____
_____
_____
_____

Mahalo,

Figure C–11. Conference letter to parents.

© 2001 from *Elevating Expectations*. Portsmouth, NH: Heinemann.

Bibliography

Ames, Cheryl K., and Hilary S. Gahagan. 1995. "Self-Reflection: Supporting Students in Taking Ownership of Evaluation." In *Who Owns Learning? Questions of Autonomy, Choice, and Control*, edited by Curt Dudley-Marling and Dennis Searle. Portsmouth, NH: Heinemann.

Au, Kathryn, Jacquelin Carroll, and Judith Scheu. 1997. *Balanced Literacy Instruction: A Teacher's Resource Book*. Norwood, MA: Christopher-Gordon.

Bridges, Lois. 1995. *Assessment, Continuous Learning*. Los Angeles, CA: The Galef Institute and York, ME: Stenhouse.

Brooks, Jacqueline G., and Martin G. Brooks. 1993, 1999. *In Search of Understanding: The Case for Constructivist Classrooms*. Alexandria, VA: Association for Supervision and Curriculum Development.

Clay, Marie. 1993. *An Observation Survey of Early Literacy Achievement*. Portsmouth, NH: Heinemann.

Davies, Anne. 2000. *Making Classroom Assessment Work*. Merville, BC: Connections.

Davies, Anne, Caren Cameron, Colleen Politano, and Kathleen Gregory. 1992. *Together Is Better*. Winnipeg, MB: Peguis.

Dewey, John. 1938, 1963. *Experience and Education*. New York: Macmillan.

Falk, Beverly. 2000. *The Heart of the Matter*. Portsmouth, NH: Heinemann.

Farr, Roger, and Bruce Tone. 1994. *Portfolio and Performance Assessment: Helping Students Evaluate Their Progress as Readers and Writers*. Forth Worth, TX: Harcourt Brace.

Finn, Chester E. Jr., Michael J. Petrilli, and Gregg Vanourek. November 1998. "Commentary: The State of State Standards. Four Reasons Why Most Don't Cut the Mustard." *Education Week* (11): 39, 56.

Fletcher, Ralph. 1993. *What a Writer Needs*. Portsmouth. NH: Heinemann.

Gardner, Howard. 1983. *Frames of Mind: The Theory of Multiple Intelligences*. New York: Basic Books.

Goodman, Yetta, Dorothy Watson, and Carolyn Burke. 1987. *Reading Miscue Inventory*. Katonah, NY: Richard C. Owen.

Goodrich, Heidi. 1997. "Understanding Rubrics." *Educational Leadership* 54 (4): 14–17.

Graves, Donald H. 1983. *Writing: Teachers and Children at Work*. Portsmouth, NH: Heinemann.

———. 1994. *A Fresh Look at Writing*. Portsmouth, NH: Heinemann.

Graves, Donald H., and Bonnie Sunstein, eds. 1992. *Portfolio Portraits*. Portsmouth, NH: Heinemann.

Gregory, Kathleen, Caren Cameron, and Anne Davies. 1997. *Setting and Using Criteria*. Merville, BC: Connections.

Hansen, Jane. 1998. *When Learners Evaluate*. Portsmouth, NH: Heinemann.

Hart, Diane. 1994. *Authentic Assessment: A Handbook for Educators*. Menlo Park, CA: Addison-Wesley.

Hawaii Department of Education. 1999. *Hawaii Content and Performance Standards II: Language Arts*. Honolulu: Hawaii Department of Education.

Hill, Bonnie C., and Cynthia A. Ruptic. 1994. *Practical Aspects of Authentic Assessment: Putting the Pieces Together*. Norwood, MA: Christopher-Gordon.

Kohn, Alfie. 1999. *The Schools Our Children Deserve: Moving Beyond Traditional Classrooms and Tougher Standards*. New York: Houghton Mifflin.

———. 2000. *The Case Against Standardized Testing*. Portsmouth, NH: Heinemann.

Ohanian, Susan. 1999. *One Size Fits Few. The Folly of Educational Standards*. Portsmouth, NH: Heinemann.

Peterson, Ralph, and Maryann Eeds. 1990. *Grand Conversations: Literature Groups in Action*. New York: Scholastic.

Piaget, Jean. 1954. *The Construction of Reality in the Child*. New York: Basic Books.

Politano, Colleen, and Anne Davies. 1994. *Multi-Age and More*. Winnipeg, MB: Peguis.

Pukui, Mary Kawena. 1983. *'Olelo no'eau: Hawaiian Proverbs and Poetical Sayings*. Honolulu, HI: Bishop Museum Press.

Rosenblatt, Louise M. 1993. "The Literary Transaction: Evocation and Response." In *Journeying: Children Responding to Literature*, edited by K. Holland, R. Hungeford, and S. Ernst. Portsmouth, NH: Heinemann.

Routman, Regie. 1991, 1994. *Invitations: Changing as Teachers and Learners K–12*, Portsmouth, NH: Heinemann.

———. 2000. *Conversations: Strategies for Teaching, Learning, and Evaluating*. Portsmouth, NH: Heinemann.

Short, Kathy. 1997. *Literature as a Way of Knowing*. Los Angeles, CA: The Galef Institute and York, ME: Stenhouse.

Short, Kathy, Jerome Harste, and Carolyn Burke. 1996. *Creating Classrooms for Authors and Inquirers*. Portsmouth, NH: Heinemann.

Smith, Frank. 1984. "Twelve Easy Ways to Make Learning to Read Difficult" in *Essays into Literacy*. Portsmouth. NH: Heinemann.

Stiggins, Richard. 1997. *Student-Centered Classroom Assessment*. Upper Saddle River, NJ: Prentice Hall.

Strickland, Kathleen, and James Strickland. 2000. *Making Assessment Elementary*. Portsmouth, NH: Heinemann.

Tierney, Robert J., Mark A. Carter, and Laura E. Desai. 1991. *Portfolio Assessment in the Reading-Writing Classroom*. Norwood, MA: Christopher-Gordon.

Valencia, Sheila, Elfrieda Hiebert, and Peter Afflerbach, eds. 1993. *Authentic Reading Assessment: Practices and Possibilities*. Newark, DE: International Reading Association.

Vygotsky, Lev. 1978. *Mind and Society*. Cambridge, MA: Harvard University Press.